Early Praise for *A Common Pornography* by Kevin Sampsell

"This is a heartbreaking and magnificent book. I love its mosaic structure—a portrait of a family and a young man created out of jewel-like fragments of memory. In its depiction of small-town American life—the ennui and despair and beauty—I am reminded of Denis Johnson's *Jesus' Son*. This is the kind of book where you want to thank the author for helping you feel less alone with being alive."

> —Jonathan Ames, author of *Wake Up, Sir!* and *The Double Life Is Twice as Good*

"For beauty, honesty, sheer weirdness, and a haunting evocation of place, Kevin Sampsell is my favorite Oregon writer. Ken Kesey, Chuck Palahniuk—make some room on the shelf."

> —Sean Wilsey, author of *Oh the Glory of It All*

"Embarrassing and honest, heartbreaking and hilarious. *A Common Pornography* is a great memoir from one of the Northwest's best writers."

> —Willy Vlautin, author of *Northline* and *The Motel Life*

"Memory and truth are jagged things, and Kevin Sampsell's memoir-in-vignettes expresses this forcefully. With grit and candor, he marches us through the heartbreak, horniness, and confusion of a West coast boy becoming a man."

> —Robin Romm, author of *The Mercy Papers*

"Kevin Sampsell's stories are brief incantations, uppercuts to the gut, prose poems given over to the bloodiest realms of the self. It's all here: the emotional squalor, the sweet bite of loneliness. Make no mistake: Sampsell can write like hell."

> —Steve Almond, author of *Candyfreak* and *My Life in Heavy Metal*

A **Common** Pornography

also by **Kevin Sampsell**

Creamy Bullets
Beautiful Blemish
How to Lose Your Mind with the Lights On
The Insomniac Reader (editor)
Portland Noir (editor)

A **Common** Pornography

a memoir

Kevin Sampsell

HARPER ● PERENNIAL

NEW YORK ● LONDON ● TORONTO ● SYDNEY ● NEW DELHI ● AUCKLAND

HARPER ● PERENNIAL

P.S.™ is a trademark of HarperCollins Publishers.

HarperCollins books may be purchased for educational, business, or sales promotional use. For information please write: Special Markets Department, HarperCollins Publishers, 10 East 53rd Street, New York, NY 10022.

FIRST EDITION

Designed by Joy O'Meara

Library of Congress Cataloging-in-Publication Data is available upon request.

ISBN 978-0-06-176610-7

10 11 12 13 14   OV/RRD   10 9 8 7 6 5 4 3 2 1

Author's Note

Some parts of this memoir were previously published in 2003 as a limited edition sixty-page book, also called *A Common Pornography*. It was written as a kind of memory experiment. A gathering of recollections from my small-town youth. Many people who read it told me they wanted to read more. I started to write more of these little vignettes, even though I wasn't sure if I would actually publish a longer version of the book.

Then, in March 2008, my father died and I went back up to Kennewick, Washington, for his funeral. I was there for four days, looking through dusty boxes of photos, letters, documents, and odd memorabilia. There was no room for me to sleep at my mom's house so one of my older brothers, Russell, let me stay with him in a nearby hotel room. Russell, and most of the other relatives who were in town for the funeral, are people I don't know very well. Russell and Gary are my two oldest half brothers; along with my oldest sibling, my half sister, Elinda, they were not around as I was growing up. I stayed up late with Russell on my last night there, talking about Dad and hearing stories I'd never heard before.

That night, and the following day when my mother and I had a long private conversation, I discovered disturbing threads of my family history and realized I needed to write about them. Although it started as a book about myself, I wanted to pull back and get a wider view. I conducted interviews with my mom, brothers, and, perhaps most important, my sister, Elinda, who spoke frankly about things other people would not want to face. In some parts of the book, I state the specific thoughts and feelings of those people. This is not conjecture on my part. It is the recollected truth, as gathered through these interviews.

Introduction

In August 2008, I had a panic attack that forced me out of my home naked. It was three thirty in the morning. I was startled awake with the feeling of something holding me down in bed. I was in my apartment alone. My fourteen-year-old son was staying at his mother's house that night. I looked around my bedroom as my eyes adjusted to the dark. My closet door was open, and a heap of dirty laundry was spilling out of it. I felt like something was standing there, watching me, ready to hurt me. Maybe it was my father. I tried to yell or scream, but I couldn't fill my throat with air and the sound came out hoarse and hollow like it does sometimes when I have bad dreams.

I kicked the blankets off and pushed myself out of bed. I turned on the lights and cautiously looked around my apartment, shaking and fearful. I paced around and thought about getting back in bed but I couldn't go back into the bedroom. I thought about calling someone, but I didn't want to wake anyone up. Plus, my phone was in the bedroom. I felt trapped and decided that I needed to leave my apartment. I grabbed the car keys and tried to go back into the bedroom to grab some clothes. I made myself speak, to see if anyone else was there and also to simply break the dull silence. "Hey," I said. And then louder, "Hey!"

There was a short echo that brought more panic into my chest and I turned and ran out the door.

I got in my car and started it. I didn't have my phone, my wallet, or any clothes. I drove around the quiet streets for a while. A few times I drove past early-morning commuters, driving slowly with their headlights on, sipping coffee from their travel mugs, half asleep and unaware that a scared, naked man debated whether or not to plow into them with his car like a missile.

I knew I needed help, but I didn't want to go to a hospital. If you go to an emergency room naked, what do they do? I wondered. I decided to go to my friend Lynne's house. She woke up, dazed and probably wondering if she was dreaming. She tried to calm me down, but I couldn't stop shaking and whipping my head around, like someone was sneaking up on me. She started a bath for me and gave me an anxiety pill. She covered me with blankets as the tub filled and I was telling her, as if giving her instructions, "The books [this book and an anthology I was editing] are on my computer. My will is in one of my yearbooks." I felt like I was cracking apart, drowning in an ocean, losing a long battle.

When I got into the tub my body started convulsing. Lynne was in her kitchen trying to find something and I felt deserted for a moment. I began wailing and crying uncontrollably. I felt possessed by a demon, both awful and sad. Maybe this, six months after the fact, was how I grieved for Dad. Maybe his ghost said, *You haven't grieved for me properly.* He didn't care that I didn't want to grieve for him or that I felt like I didn't have to. He was going to make me, even if it was against my will.

A **Common** Pornography

Washington Street

Dad came home and went straight upstairs to the bedroom I shared with my older brother Matt. "I'm going to throw everything into the middle of the street," he yelled. He would get mad when the house wasn't clean. His brown work shoe tapped the side of our small television, making the picture flicker. I imagined the traffic on our busy street, dodging our piles of clothes, destroying our dressers, spraying chunks of broken dishes everywhere.

Matt and I had grass stains from playing Nerf football all day. There was a bowl of melted Neapolitan ice cream sitting next to my bed, near a pile of clothes and some comics.

This kind of scenario happened more than once.

I was the youngest. Two of my older brothers lived there in the house still, but all the others—two half brothers who seemed like myth and a half sister—had walked through similar emotions and trials already. They were free somewhere in the world.

Egg Hunt

When the gun sounded, Matt ran ahead of me with the other kids who filled the park. I could tell they were all excited, yelling into the wet spring air. The sky was speckled with birds and high dark clouds. I ran the other way, back toward home.

When I got to the house, Mom held me as I cried for no good reason. My brother came in the side door with his homemade Superman cape over his shoulder and a basket of decorated eggs and chocolate candies. It was the first time I gave up.

Attractions

I thought Kennewick was the ideal place to grow up. Of course, this was before I even saw anywhere else.

My favorite attraction was the Cable Bridge. I remember the kind of awe and joy that only an eleven-year-old can muster about such an object. When the bridge opened for traffic in 1978, it seemed almost unbelievable that this was the first cable-stayed bridge in the country. Dad drove our family across on the first day it opened. My other brother who still lived in the house, Mark, was with Matt and me in the backseat. We craned our necks to look out the back window and watched the cables slanting to the high columns in the middle of the bridge. We didn't have any tall buildings or other interesting structures at all in the Tri-Cities and this first impression was breathtaking. It made me think of the Golden Gate Bridge in San Francisco, which I knew only from pictures. I thought the Cable Bridge, which connects Kennewick to Pasco, was the coolest thing I'd ever seen in person. It was a majestic backdrop for the yearly hydroplane races, which were also a source of hometown pride, as they were supposedly the second most well-attended hydroplane events in the country.

The only other interesting creation in the area was the

Wet 'n Wild water park, which opened up by the Columbia Center Mall when I was a teenager. It also had some important-sounding rank among national attractions. It supposedly had the third longest water slides in the country. Going down those slippery tubes rubbed the hair off my calves and made my body feel like it was full of static electricity. Then I had to wait in line for a long time, shivering and dripping, until I was back at the top. The lifeguards there were always too cool to look at anyone. They kept their eyes set on a particular curve of the slide and then waved their hand lazily, signaling the sliders to go. For some reason, it was closed down a few years later and then eventually demolished to make room for a car dealership.

Elinda

Elinda is my mother's first child, born in 1946.

Elinda's father was with my mother for only a brief time, physically abusing her and then disappearing for a long time after he was sent away for an armed robbery in Great Falls, Montana.

Shortly after that, Mom met a man named Jimmy and they got married. Elinda was afraid of Jimmy and would have nightmares about him, even after Mom had two children with him—Gary and Russell.

Mom and Jimmy got divorced when Elinda was five.

My dad came into the picture in 1956. He wanted to help Mom with the children, but he was often overwhelmed trying to provide for them. Despite their struggles, he wanted to have his own children. My brother Mark was born in 1960.

When Elinda was a little girl, she would often daydream in school and her teacher thought she was mentally retarded, or, as they called it back then, "feebleminded."

Mom was wrestling with her own health concerns. She was epileptic and would have seizures quite often, shaking the whole house, scaring the kids, and waking up unsure of what was happening to her. It took several years and several treatments to get the right medicine to stop the attacks.

When my sister, Elinda, became a teenager, she was sent to Medical Lake, a psychiatric hospital, from 1960 to 1970. When she began there, she weighed ninety-eight pounds. Two years later, she weighed two hundred. She became diabetic.

While she was there, she received eight shock treatments. After each treatment, she would sit somewhere and wonder, *Why can't I think?*

She was sexually active in the hospital and became pregnant after having sex with one of the other inmates on the concrete floor of the mailroom. She wanted to get married to this person and have a life outside of the hospital with him, but when she had the baby, a healthy boy, the hospital officials deemed her unfit to be a mother. The child was immediately taken from her before she could see it.

Reasons

There was an old woman at Medical Lake with Elinda. She was like a grandmother to everyone and would play pinochle with Elinda. She was in there for killing her husband and children. Another woman had drowned her kids. Those were reasons for being there, Elinda thought. Those women had even sent warnings and when those warnings were ignored, they did what they said they were going to do.

Another woman who spent time at the hospital while Elinda lived there was my dad's sister, Evelyn. She was battling depression and schizophrenia. But oddly, they weren't aware of each other.

Elinda could never come up with a clear, solid reason why she was there in the first place. No specific label or complicated acronym. "The simple way of expressing what I could have had is *crazy*," she has told me. "But they wouldn't label me crazy. I've got to fight my brain all the time now."

When she left, she was worse than when she entered.

Saved

Matt told me a story once about how I almost got lost at the Medical Lake hospital when I was four. We had gone with Mom to visit Elinda and he was supposed to be watching me. I ran off somewhere, scampering around corners, hiding behind doors, trying not to laugh. Finally Matt found me, just before I walked into the outstretched arms of a drooling old woman in a tattered nightgown.

After Medical Lake

When Elinda turned twenty-four, she left Medical Lake and was married soon after. Joseph, her first husband, like Mom's first husband, was a terrible mistake. He drank and smoked all day long and was physically and emotionally abusive. He treated Elinda like less than an animal and accepted money from friends who wanted to have sex with her. She became pregnant with the child of one of his friends and, despite her situation, wanted to keep the baby.

Elinda and Joseph were living in Pasco at the time, not far from Mom and Dad and the rest of us, across the bridge in Kennewick. I was just a toddler.

Mom discussed Elinda's circumstances with Dad, knowing that Elinda would probably not be allowed to care for the baby herself. The baby was going to be half-black, and whether that was part of the reason or not, Dad refused to be a caregiver for another child.

When the baby, a girl, was born, Elinda was allowed to be a mother for a few days before the baby was taken away and given up for adoption.

Elinda's troubled marriage soon came to an end. Joseph became more violent than usual and kicked her front teeth out and broke her nose. He told her that if she didn't leave, he was going to kill her. So she left.

She served him with divorce papers after that, wanting to cut him out of her life, but he didn't file the papers properly and thirty years later, after he died, she found out that they were never legally divorced.

Bird Whistles

One of my earliest memories of Elinda is the bird whistle trick. Matt and I had these plastic whistles that were shaped like birds. You would put water in them and blow into a hole by their tails and it would sound like the fluttering tweet of a bird. My sister was sitting on the front porch of our house, watching the traffic on Washington Street or maybe squinting at the giant neon cross of the Nazarene church across from us. Matt and I would hide around the corner and blow on the whistles. Elinda would whip her head around and shout, "Where's that bird at? Birdie? Birdie birdie?"

Dad saw us through the window and shook his head. Mom finally came out and told us to knock it off.

Bedbugs

Elinda stayed with us sometimes at our house. She would sleep on the couch. One night, she awoke at 3:30 a.m. and felt Dad touching her. He didn't say anything but she could smell alcohol on his breath. She didn't know what to do and thought for a moment that maybe she was dreaming. The house was quiet and she felt paralyzed. He climbed on top of her. She decided that she could not scream because she didn't want to wake up any of us kids.

I was probably four at the time. Matt and Mark and I were sleeping upstairs. I remember that every night in that house, Mom would tuck me in and say, "Good night." Then I'd answer, "Sleep tight." Then she'd say, "Don't let the bedbugs bite." We would repeat this, back and forth, even as she left my room and walked back down the stairs. Her voice answering my voice until I stopped saying, "Sleep tight."

"Don't let the bedbugs bite."

I did not know about what happened between Elinda and Dad until the day after his funeral. Mom wanted to have some one-on-one talks with her kids before we all scattered again. So she and I ended up at a new Sonic drive-in. We ordered root beer floats and for the first time ever, we spoke openly about the dysfunctions of the family.

She told me more about her first husbands, about Elinda's childhood, about why she stayed with Dad, even though it was evident that there was little love from him.

I felt bad for Mom because, in a way, it seemed like she was apologizing on behalf of Dad for not being a good father. When she told me the story about him and Elinda, it answered one question I had always had: Why was there no affection displayed in our family? Now I understood that she was disgusted. The kind of disgust that flowed through our bloodline and poisoned everyone in our house.

Dad had made Elinda pregnant on that night.

Last Man

Elinda went to Yakima and got an abortion after that. She came back to our house a few weeks later. Nobody knew where she had gone or that she had been pregnant. She knew that she had to tell someone, so she told Mom. I believe this was the moment when all of Mom's affection for Dad disappeared. After that, Dad constantly became angry at Elinda. The sort of anger that was made up of jealousy, resentment, and embarrassment. He started to blame her for every little thing that went wrong—a broken wiper on the truck, a mess in the kitchen, the heat being turned up too high. Then once, late at night when they were alone again, Dad went over and sat next to Elinda on the couch. He put his arm around her and told her he loved her and wanted to marry her. She told him, "You can remove your hand, and I wouldn't marry you if you were the last man on earth."

One P, Another L

The family name was originally spelled Samsel. Some time in the 1930s, when my dad was a kid, his mother changed it slightly, adding the *P* and extra *L*. Apparently, someone named Samsel had committed some terrible crime that summer and she didn't want her kids going to school with that name.

Spirits

Two of the neighborhood kids, Willie and Todd, joined my brother Matt and me in a game we had invented. We'd make a quick buzzing sound and become a "spirit," which was like a superhero. There were good guy spirits and bad guy spirits, and each one had a special power.

Matt's main spirit, The Claw, had a dangerous weapon called the Brain Hold. There was no defense against this hold but Matt was fair by not doing it all the time. He'd often yell, "Brain Hold!" whenever he was going to do it. I had one spirit that was so fast he could run around the house several times and not look like he was moving at all. I had to tell my friends when he was done running. I imagined that this spirit might have a female sidekick, but there were no girls who would play with us. Todd's sister was about our age, but we all teased her because she wasn't pretty and her name was Sissy.

At night, in our bedroom, Matt and I would talk about what our spirits were going to do next, and discuss maybe killing off some of our old spirits for new ones. It was highly dramatized and loosely scripted, like the professional wrestling we watched on Saturdays. The show, *Big Time Wrestling*, was a weekly ritual for us. This was before wrestling became glitzy and hugely marketed. Some of the popular Northwest wrestlers like "Playboy" Buddy Rose, Jimmy Snuka, Jesse Ventura, and "Rowdy" Roddy Piper even came to Kennewick and wrestled at the high school sometimes.

I was going to make up a spirit with a super brain to combat The Claw and his famous hold, but Willie and Todd moved away and we stopped playing.

That's when Matt and I began reading books about Bigfoot.

Records

Two plastic record players and a nice stack of Top 40
45s were all I needed to start my own radio station. My plan
was to do a pirate radio show that would broadcast to my
neighborhood. Instead I just pointed my speakers out the
upstairs window and hoped the sound reached the corner.

In fifth grade I started writing really bad pop song lyrics. When I wrote something I thought to be particularly
hit-worthy, I'd cut out a piece of paper in the shape of a 45,
and then, after coloring in the black wax area, I'd put the
name of my song on the "label." Some of these hits were
"Sound of Thunder," "Rich Dude," and "Diamond Girl."
The name I gave myself was Billy Rivers, because I thought
it sounded cool.

After cutting out the center hole, I'd string the smash
hit to a hook on my ceiling. I imagined I was a megastar.
Sometimes I'd even put them on one of the turntables and
watch them spin. Forty-five revolutions per minute. Once
I put a needle on one as it spun and ruined the needle. I
had to go to the record store, where they sold little smoking
pipes and stoner posters, spending my entire five-dollar al-
lowance on a new snap-on needle.

OK 95

The popular radio station was OK 95. They hosted a discount at the River-Vue Drive-In movie once and I went with a bunch of friends and one of their parents. We loaded up a station wagon full of people and got in for ninety-five cents. Some people from the radio station were giving out records as we drove in. My friends and I stuck our heads out the windows to see what they had. There were a couple of boxes full of albums, but it was all stuff we had never heard of. They were probably rejects, bands from small labels that sent their records to the station in hopes of getting their big break. A dozen cars behind us started to get impatient, revving their engines and honking their horns, but we didn't know what to take. Finally, the radio station people gave each of us a random record. They all looked suspiciously like hard rock, which OK 95 wasn't playing at the time. I ended up with a record by Krokus. It was called *Hardware*. When I listened to it later, I was repulsed by the music—a tasteless sort of stoner metal. There was one song in particular called "Smelly Nelly" that talked about a girl's crotch. It has the worst lyrics ever ("Her skin is dry and spotty but her ass is just the best"). I'm sure OK 95 was glad to be rid of all those records.

Wet

At halftime of the high school football game, Dad and I walked down the bleachers and waited for our turn in the bathroom. There was a long urinal where about six people could go at once. Dad and I went side by side and he seemed to be watching me as I pulled my pants down to my knees and went.

When we were back outside, standing in line to get hot dogs, he explained to me that I didn't have to pull my pants down to pee. He pointed to our zippers, showing me how they were made to open up so just our peters came out. I felt embarrassed, not realizing that people were probably staring at me in there, wondering why I had to pull my pants all the way down. I believe I was eleven at this time. I wore tight white briefs and probably didn't change them enough. Soon after this talk, I also stopped wetting my bed at night.

J. V. Cain

In 1979, two years after I became a big football fan, J. V. Cain, the starting tight end of my favorite team, the Cardinals, died suddenly in training camp. It was the first time I felt shocked by a death. He died on his twenty-sixth birthday. I rode my bike to the drug store every day that week to read the national newspapers to see if they figured out what the cause was.

There was one particular J. V. Cain touchdown that I'll never forget. It was against the Browns in a close game. He ran a simple ten-yard hook pattern to the goal line and turned to catch. The ball was overthrown but J. V. reached up with a larger-than-life right hand and pulled it down like he was tearing a bird out of the sky. It seemed unbelievable.

The drug store kept their newspapers by the magazine rack, away from the busy cash register area, so it was easy for me to tear through the sports section every day without the clerk shooing me away. I read multiple papers, speculated with friends, and even asked the family doctor about what would cause such a bewildering death. Eventually it was announced as a heart attack. The team retired Cain's jersey number 88 and wore black armbands that season, which turned out to be another terrible one.

Silhouette

Matt and I saw a spaceship skipping through the sky. We reacted at the same time, surprised we both saw it. We stayed up late that night, sleeping outside on our side porch in our sleeping bags. We talked about UFOs and Bigfoot. We planned a Bigfoot hunt near Walla Walla when we got older.

After falling asleep, exhausted from speculation, I awoke sometime in the middle of the night. Unsure why I was dream-interrupted, I lifted my head to look around. Roughly twenty yards away, near the alley and beside the garbage cans, stood a large figure with its legs slightly spread and its arms at its sides. It was a silhouette similar to that on a men's room door. We had a dog at the time, a shaggy black mutt named Pebbles who was about the size of a breadbox. He was looking at the figure too, but he didn't make a sound. I froze and kept my eyes on the figure. It seemed to be watching Matt and me sleep.

The next morning we called the radio station to see if there were other sightings of a strange light in the sky. There were. We talked about it all morning until Dad got agitated and told us to zip our mouths. I'm pretty sure that Dad believed in UFOs too, so I was surprised he got angry. It was probably against the Bible for Catholics to openly believe in UFOs or something. I never got around to mentioning the shadowy figure by the garbage cans. I thought maybe I was dreaming.

Almost ten years later, while discussing that night with Matt, he told me he had seen the same silhouette, and that's why he never wanted to sleep outside again.

Black

My brother Matt is black. We have the same mother but little was known about his father, who was an African man named Everest Mulekezi. Our mother dated Everest for a short time after meeting him at a dance in Eastern Washington. He was a foreign student attending Washington State University.

Mom and Dad had split up at this time, though they would eventually get back together and have me a couple years later.

There was only one other black kid in our neighborhood. His name was Larry, and we were friends with him for a while. One time Matt and Larry got into a fight about something though, and Larry called my brother a "half breed."

Just two weeks later, Larry drowned in the Columbia River. We went to his funeral at a black church in Pasco. His family became hysterical. I think it was his sister who started screaming and had to be taken away. We left early.

When Matt turned thirty-five, he decided to look for his father. His search took him to Africa, where he met several family members but learned that his father had died in 1971 in Uganda. He was some sort of a district official who was executed by Idi Amin's army after a dispute over a hotel bill. The rest of Everest's family was hunted as well, but most of them escaped.

There was an odd moment during his African trip that Matt told me about. He had just met his real father's sister for the first time and many of his other relatives were coming to her apartment to meet him. As he sat and talked and got buzzed on a terrible-tasting local brew consisting of smashed up bananas and alcohol, he realized that his newfound relatives were watching him extra close, almost studying him. Matt asked them if something was wrong. They paused and then smiled and told Matt that he did indeed display parts of his father. He had his dad's mannerisms and his determination. Physically they could see Everest in Matt's eyes, forehead, and hands. Though he never knew his father in life, Matt had been carrying his ghost for all these years. He felt this ghost become more a part of him now, and with his family circled around him, he began to weep.

Cherokee Pride

Matt and I played out some game while listening to one of our favorite 45s, "Indian Reservation" by Paul Revere and the Raiders. We would take turns playing the roles. One of us would be the sad and angry Indian in jail while the other was the guard. Around this time was when the TV commercial with the crying Indian was so popular— the anti-littering one.

"Indian Reservation" was one of the biggest hits for this band of white guys who dressed in pirate outfits. It seemed to have this great dramatic sense of impending revenge that pulsed just behind the drumbeat and the heartfelt sentiment of the singer/narrator. It was like a story song. The chorus went something like: "Cherokee people, Cherokee tribe / So proud to live, so proud to die."

Sometimes at the end of the song we'd pretend to fight, and one day we actually did. He was twisting my arm really hard and I threw a wild punch at his groin. It was the only time I ever hurt him.

Scratchmuback

As far as I can tell, I am the itchiest person in the world. I think it started when I was a small kid and started to demand back scratching from Mom. Every day for probably too many years, often multiple times a day, I would sit on Mom's lap and say, "Scratch my back." But it was more like one word: Scratchmuback. She never tired of doing it and probably spoiled me for all my future girlfriends, many of whom did in fact say that I was the itchiest person in the world. Many of my itches are in places that I can easily reach, but I still get a strange pleasure from asking someone to scratch my elbow, ear, or nose.

For most of my thirties, I even developed an odd patch of skin on the outside of my left nipple. It was dry and slightly scaly and scratching it gave me the greatest pleasure. I knew that it probably wasn't healthy, but I didn't want to get rid of it because that would put an end to all those moments of scratching pleasure. It was simply known as "the Patch." My girlfriends thought it was weird when I explained it to them but they reluctantly humored me when I would ask them to "Scratchmupatch."

I did try some lotions and creams, halfheartedly hoping to cure myself, but it wouldn't go away. Eventually a prescription steroid gel did the job and the Patch faded away.

Sometimes if I scratch in that same spot, I can still feel a trace of pleasure.

Grapes

Sometimes, when I was very little, we'd go to my grand-parents' house, on the other side of Kennewick. Dad's mom and dad.

They lived right across from Kamiakin High School and had several rows of impressive grape vines and a big garden. Matt and Mark and I would sometimes spend hours there, picking grapes and goofing around in their big barn. When we got hungry, Grandma would make toast and a special milk drink with malted milk powder or strawberry Quik. Grandpa always drank buttermilk. It almost made me sick to watch him drink it because it was so lumpy.

During the week, students from the high school would sit in their yard during lunch break and leave behind their trash. Grandpa told them to clean up after themselves or not sit there. Some of the kids got mad about this and began leaving more trash in the yard, sometimes in the middle of the night. One day, while talking to one of the kids, Grandpa had a heart attack and died. That was the first funeral I ever went to.

Soon after that, Grandma sold the house and property to the Welch's company, who wanted to expand the vine-yard. The house was vandalized and riddled with graffiti: spray-painted swear words and pentagrams and swastikas. A couple of years later, the land was leveled and an apartment complex was built.

Grandma lived her last years in Walla Walla, a town I hated for no good reason. But whenever we drove there to visit her, there was a big wooden sign in the shape of the Jolly Green Giant that Matt and I thought was cool. We mimicked the jingle ("Ho ho ho—Green Giant!") and then went back to playing Slugbug.

Grandma died in Walla Walla.

Car-Mull

Jeffrey was a snot-nosed neighbor kid who was a year younger than me. He hadn't even reached the wisdom of a double-digit age. My brother Matt seemed ancient and stoic at the ripe age of fourteen by comparison. I looked up to him and any kid who was older than eleven. Matt always seemed older than he actually was.

Once we told Jeffrey that all the bird poop on our car was caramel. We sat on the hood and pretended to pinch some in our fingers. We brought our fingers up to our lips and pretended to chew and smack our lips. We were convincing and Jeffrey smeared some onto his tongue. "Where does it come from?" he asked.

We told him that when rain drips from certain trees, it becomes caramel.

"My mom won't let me eat caramel," he said. He pronounced it "car-mull."

"We won't tell her if you don't," I said.

Fights

Sometimes Mom and Dad got into unexplainable fights. I wasn't sure where the tension was coming from at the time. (I'm sure what happened with Elinda had something to do with it, but I had no idea about that yet.) Dad had typical gripes, like Mom not having dinner ready on time. Sometimes Mom would question Dad about staying at the bar too long after work. I remember him saying, "They kept buying me drinks. What am I supposed to do, say no?"

My dad had a quick temper and things escalated without warning. There were fists thrown, choke holds, objects broken. I would go to my room and jump into bed, crying and pressing my head into the pillows to mute the noise, though I still felt it pounding like an earthquake through the walls. Sometimes Matt would do the same thing.

Eventually, when we were older and bigger, there was a time when Matt got fed up with the fights and decided to do something. He stepped between them and pressed Dad against the wall, his strong arm under Dad's chin, and told him, "You're not going to talk to Mom like that. You're not going to hit her again." Dad's body was tensed and surprised at Matt's strength. He started to panic and asked Matt to let him go. After that, he never got mad when Matt was around. He became more passive. He looked at Matt sometimes with eyes that shyly asked, *Are we okay? Is everything cool between us?*

Centerfolds

Todd's family lived right across the alley behind us. His dad was always working on his race car in their garage, and it was the loudest thing in the neighborhood. He raced it at the local speedway and in other cities too. Sometimes I'd go in there and ask if Todd was around and his dad would let me cut through their backyard to get to the front of their house. The reason I liked going into the garage most, though, was because Todd's dad had a bunch of *Playboy* centerfolds up on the walls. I remember seeing *Playboy* centerfolds in other people's garages too. But there were pictures from other magazines as well. Women wearing bikinis or torn shirts and leaning on motorcycles or across the hood of a hot rod. Maybe having all those naked women around helped Todd's dad feel better about all the time he worked on his car.

One time when I was over at Todd's, I had to use the bathroom and walked in while his mom was in the shower. I stopped for a second and started to back out. But then I realized that she didn't know I was in there. She was on the other side of these thick and blurry shower doors. I saw her warped image as she rubbed the water and shampoo into her hair, the shape of her body out of focus. It felt like my bladder was about to burst, but I stared for a long time while holding it in.

Chongo

The toughest kid at our school was named Chongo, and he was a short but muscular Mexican who always seemed to be suspended or doing Saturday school. He lived in the pit of this valley that ran alongside a long irrigation pipe. The pipe was connected to the ditches surrounding our neighborhood and it had a flat surface on top lined with flimsy two-by-fours. For some reason, we always called this pipe "the floons." My friends and I would often have races on the floons. There was an element of danger whenever we did because there were big gaps where you could fall through and go into the dirty water. And if we went too far down the floons we'd be dangerously close to what we called "Chongo Country." Other kids had told us that if you got a good look into Chongo Country, you'd see all sorts of stolen bikes and bike parts in his weed-filled yard. When Chongo had his shirt off, they said, you could see a tattoo of Pontius Pilate across his chest. We never dared to look.

Field Trip

Mom served up a hundred hot dogs and then helped someone bandage his hand after he hurt it with a fire-cracker. She often volunteered to help with my fifth grade outings.

Summer vacation was just an hour away.

All the kids got back on the bus to head back to school. We had spent the day at Sacajawea Park. Mom was missing. I asked my teacher and she said she didn't know where she was.

Driving up Washington Street on the bus, I noticed smoke billowing up somewhere in my neighborhood. Seconds later I was yelling at the bus driver to stop. I saw the firefighters spraying at the flames that came out of my bedroom window. The driver said he wasn't allowed to let me out. When we got back to school, a friend's mother drove me to my house, which was badly burned on the top and on the sides by our upstairs bedrooms. Mom had left the field trip early and was home already, watching the tall flames from a neighbor's driveway. The cause was unknown but I heard someone imply that my older brother Mark was home from school, smoking pot (I'd seen him and his friends smoke pot once and thought it looked cool—there was this twisted glass thing they used).

We stood outside watching. Nobody was hurt. My dad was in the alley screaming, "Fuck the world!"

It seemed like a lot of people were watching the house become wrecked with fire and water, and when they grew bored of it, they went back home.

Interim

On our first night after the fire, we stayed with a family from our church. They were trying to conserve water and I remember taking a bath with one of their boys before bed. The next couple of days we stayed at a motel in Pasco while the insurance matters were figured out. We spent part of those days going through our stuff at the house, figuring out what was too trashed (burned or water damaged) to keep. We stored all the salvageable things in our garage, which was just a cluttered mess of a structure made out of concrete, tin, and mismatched wood.

A few days later, we found a basement apartment to live in and we started moving our stuff over. It was only a block away, which was convenient, but besides that, it was way too small and depressing. The main problem was that it didn't have windows. Living there made me feel like I was in solitary confinement. Or "family confinement." A friend asked me if we lived in a bomb shelter.

The June sun was unbearably hot and everyone was sweaty as we carried boxes of stuff down the alley to our temporary home. Toward the end of the day, Matt and I tried to help Dad move the refrigerator down the concrete steps to the apartment. Halfway down, Dad's fingers got slippery and he smashed them on the guardrail. "Fuckshit-godfuckcockbitchfuck!" he yelled.

It was the most inspired stream of bad language Matt or I had ever heard and we would repeat it often for the next few years. We had that George Carlin record where he said the "seven words you can't say on television," but that routine paled in comparison to this.

Mayfair

Darren Green was one of my best friends. His grandparents lived next to us, so I saw him only every few weeks when he visited them. But we became best friends and always talked about what it would be like when we got older and moved into a loft apartment together. One of our favorite things to do was go to Dairy Queen and get sundaes in those plastic football helmets. We did that for a few football seasons, trying to collect the helmets of all the teams.

Another thing we did was look at dirty magazines. We discovered that the guys' employee bathroom at the Mayfair Market was a good place to look. Even though we lived right across the street, we would sometimes use the bathroom there, and we'd usually find a *Playboy* or *Penthouse* poorly hidden behind the garbage can.

We were just becoming familiar with naked women since the Dinken brothers had shown us some of the hardcore magazines their dad kept behind the seat of his old pickup. I'd steal candy bars for those Dinken kids, and, in exchange, they'd tear out pages from the magazines for me. The pictures were often of couples, and those confused me more than anything. Just naked women standing by themselves were all Darren and I needed.

Once, at the Mayfair, I talked Darren into stealing one

of the magazines by stuffing it down his pants. On his way out of the store it slid out of his left pant leg, and he was taken to the manager's office. I ran across the street and watched the store to see if he'd get away. Minutes later, police arrived. Then his parents. I was scared they were talking about me.

The Manships

Another family in the neighborhood was the Manships. Carl and Kenny were the kids and they seemed really poor and depressed. Carl was my age and Kenny was a couple years younger. Their parents were old and mean. The dad always wore dirty overalls as if he farmed all day (maybe he did, I don't know) and the mom was an apron-wearing biddy with varicose veins everywhere. I thought she had some kind of disease.

Their house was really small and dusty. They had a tiny front yard with a little grass, but their backyard was all hard dirt and dog shit. An old Ford truck from the forties or fifties sat near the alley with weeds growing around it. Matt and I would play games with Carl and Kenny sometimes, but we never hung out at their place, mainly because they had a crappy TV—an old black-and-white one that picked up only three channels. And the only snacks they had were hard candies that were all stuck together in a glass bowl.

If we were ever out playing somewhere, it would always have to be in the neighborhood, because Carl and Kenny's dad would never leave his yard to look for them. He would only bark out their names in a voice that sounded like extra-chunky gravel. It would grow harsher, louder, and more curt with each call. If Carl and Kenny weren't within shouting distance, we were pretty sure they'd get their dad's belt.

Mark

My brother Mark had moved into a small house with a friend shortly after the house fire. He had just graduated high school and was cooking at a hotel restaurant. People thought the hotel was kind of fancy because it was on a piece of land that jutted out into the Columbia River. It was called Clover Island.

Some people still thought he had something to do with the house fire, but nothing was ever proven.

Every time I went to the new house that he lived in, it smelled of thick pot smoke and thin beer. Mark was also becoming more interested in motorcycles at this time. I thought this combination of things added up to being a Hells Angel or something. Dad didn't like me going over there because he probably knew what was going on.

One night though, I made up some kind of story and went over there to watch a KISS concert on HBO. There were other people hanging out, most of them sitting on the floor as Mark and his roommate tried to figure out how to hook up the stereo speakers to the TV. About halfway through the concert, Gene Simmons began an ominous bass refrain between songs and then started spitting fake blood out of his mouth. But he wasn't really spitting. It was more like he was just letting it gurgle out of his lips and down his chin. When he was done, his stuck his long tongue out and gave a devious look as the band started into "God of Thunder." Everyone watching the concert totally loved this, except me. I thought it went too far and I was afraid I might have nightmares about the bloody face. Someone said it was a trick, that Gene kept a packet of goat's blood in the back of his mouth until it was time to bite down on it. The person who explained this said it was easy to hide stuff in your mouth. He pulled at the corner of his mouth with a finger and showed us a wad of gum stuck to one of his stained wisdom teeth.

I always liked Paul Stanley, the star-eyed guitar player and singer, better than Gene. I liked the pucker of his lips, the androgynous superhero quality that he had. Plus he owned a certain cool quality the rest of the band lacked. He would never stoop to spewing blood.

Later on, when Peter Criss stepped out from behind the mammoth cluster of drums and sat at the edge of the stage to sweetly serenade the fans with their unlikely hit "Beth," one of the floor sitters nodded at me and said something to Mark. "He's cool," Mark said. Then suddenly there was a joint being passed around.

Being "cool," I wasn't sure what was expected of me. I was maybe eleven or twelve and I hadn't even puffed a cigarette yet. When the joint was offered to me I simply passed it on to the next person. By the end of the ballad, it was so small that someone had put a tiny clamp on the thing. I started to think that the whole getting stoned thing was looking pretty desperate.

Dad never found out that I went over there to watch the

concert, but he did give me a disappointed shake of the head a few months later when I got a T-shirt with a KISS picture ironed on it. We were out at Skipper's for our Friday night fish dinner and he said, "Do you know what that means? It means Kids in Satan's Service."

Fried fish is the only food that I liked with ketchup. I squirted the thick red goo into the little paper cups and thought about the bloody face as we waited for our dinner.

Dog Days

"Have you been having bad dreams about dogs?" Mark asked me. "Because Mom and Dad said they might have to send you to a shrink or something. So you better knock it off." This was partially Mark's fault anyway, since it was his roommate's dog that bit me at their house. Three different places: leg, elbow, forearm. I shielded myself with the screen door until they got home and found me there with blood dripping on the welcome mat.

At the hospital I was given three shots. Before I left, the nurse showed me a cardboard box with little plastic toys in it. I didn't take any.

A few months later, Mom and Dad let me pick out a puppy for myself. I chose a German shepherd with floppy ears that was just a couple months old. I took Polaroids of him for the first year and a half, documenting his quick growth in our tiny apartment. His name was Scooter. He slept in my bed and I talked to him as I fell asleep each night.

Themes

In my sixth grade Social Studies class, we often read silently out of the textbook for twenty or thirty minutes at a time. My teacher, a music fan, would let us bring tapes in and play them on the cassette player while we read. It couldn't be too distracting, though, and most of the time it ended up being instrumental.

I had recently bought my first cassette recorder, a boom box the size of a toaster, and started recording songs off the radio. I didn't want to get any of the DJs' voices on my tapes so there were always clunky segues between songs. The DJs would just jabber and say dumb things before the vocals kicked in. I'd be missing the whole intro to "My Sharona" or "Heart of Glass." Then if they started talking again at the end, I'd have to cut the song there too. But my ears got used to it because that was the only way to listen to my favorite songs over and over.

My teacher played only one of my tapes for a few songs before changing it.

I turned to another passion. Theme music. First, I mail ordered an album of music from the National Football League. Found in the back of a football magazine, the ad said it featured orchestral pieces that were used by people like Howard Cosell during the football highlights they showed at halftime on *Monday Night Football*. There were a couple of songs in particular that really got me excited— "Heavy Action (Monday Night Football Theme)" by Johnny Pearson and a crazy sixties-type bebop song called "The Lineman" by Sam Spence.

I also perfected the art of recording my favorite theme songs from TV shows. I held the boom box up to the TV speaker and pleaded to the family to be quiet when the show was starting. I was partial to the cool, stylish themes like the ones from *Barney Miller, Taxi,* and *Welcome Back, Kotter.* Upbeat tunes like the ones from *Happy Days* and *The Jeffersons* were also favorites. Still, the teacher wouldn't play the tape in class because it was from TV, which represented the opposite of reading.

Pot

Chad Crouch was my first stoner friend. He lived in a ranch house with faded green paint three blocks from our middle school. There was gravel in the front yard, so his stepdad could park on it, I guess. I sometimes went there after school.

Once he pulled a bong out of a closet and showed me how to smoke pot with it. It didn't seem like he had this bong hidden very well in the closet, so I assumed his parents used it too. They were a whole family of stoners. Besides my stoner brother, I didn't know much about drugs then, just that they were bad and made you want to fly through the air like Superman.

I tried to hold the smoke in like Chad showed me but it still didn't seem to have an effect on me. Chad leaned back with half-closed eyes and said something about how high he was. He looked like a sleepy cat. I thought he was faking it.

I kept waiting for something to happen to my brain, or for my head to feel like a lost balloon, but it never happened. So I faked it a little too, just to keep him as a friend. I laughed like he laughed, at the stupidest things, so I wouldn't be a total drag.

Space Shuttle

We went to California once in a motor home to see a space shuttle land. One of my half brothers, Russell, was stationed at Edwards Air Force Base and that's where it was supposed to land. We went to some kind of NASA museum that morning before this "historic event" was to occur. Dad bought a black baseball-style cap with NASA in yellow letters on it. It was really hot out there by the landing strip and there were hundreds of people around with cameras and umbrellas. People were taking scissors and cutting the sleeves off their T-shirts. Dad got carried away and cut the whole top of his new cap off.

"My head's gotta breathe," he said. Everyone thought it was foolish, even Mom, who kind of snorted at him and said it looked silly.

We felt sorry for Dad and I think he felt sorry for himself too, because after a couple of hours he took it off and put it in the motor home.

The space shuttle landed without a hitch, but we couldn't see anything with all the people there. Later that day, I saw the cap in the motor home's trash bag.

Russell

I **always thought** that my oldest half brothers, Russell and Gary, were the favored children in the family. They were both in the military, Russell in the Air Force and Gary in the Coast Guard. I figured Dad was proud of them because they had real careers that were serious and respectable. I was never interested in joining the military, mostly because I was afraid of going to war and I hated those commercials where they said they did more before 8 a.m. than most people did in a whole day or whatever they said. Waking up so early seemed like torture to me. Plus, I didn't like being yelled at and I knew there was a lot of yelling involved.

Russell told me later that the real reason they signed up for the military after turning eighteen was to simply get away from Dad, not to earn his respect. The way he described Dad's treatment of them as his stepsons was like psychological torment. At Christmastime, Russell said my father would get him and Gary the most minimal gift possible, sometimes used toys. But for Mark, he would bring out something new and big, like a bike or guitar. He would make a big presentation of telling Mark that Gary and Russell weren't allowed to play with his gift. It turns out that, back then, Mark was like the Golden Child in the family.

Russell and Gary, the older boys, were the targets of Dad's anger and resentment. Russell said that after he earned his license and bought a car, he would often drive to his girlfriend's house and sleep in the backseat until morning, and then give her a ride to school. His car was a place to escape.

Gary

Once, when I was twelve, Gary was visiting us when a huge family fight erupted. It started with Dad and Mark at the dinner table. Mom tried to stop it and then Matt got involved too. Dad didn't like it when Matt voiced his opinion about family matters. He would sometimes try to mute Matt's presence by saying, "He's not even my kid."

Then Mark and Matt began arguing and eventually ended up outside, ready to fight. Mark called Matt a nigger and then it was a blur of arms and legs tumbling over in the middle of the yard.

Something broke in my naïve brain at that moment. I obviously knew Matt was different, but we never really voiced it. It was probably for my comfort that we ignored the difference of our skin. I thought if we talked about this difference it would create a distance and awkwardness between us. I wanted to think that other people were accepting of Matt without thinking about it too much. But in our small-town reality, he was the only black student at Kennewick High School. When he was a kid, there were signs on the bridge to Pasco that said all blacks had to be back in Pasco before a certain time. We never lived in Pasco.

I was totally unfamiliar and ignorant of what he had to deal with because of his skin color. I knew the word *nig-*

ger though, and I knew I never wanted it anywhere near my lips, though there were surely times when I was angry enough to use it. But it would be a knife I'd never be able to pull out. A bullet that would spike his heart and stay there.

Mark scrambled up and ran off somewhere down the alley. Matt walked away in the other direction. Gary came outside then and found me, stunned and alone in the yard. He spoke to me calmly but in a tone of voice that said he was leaving. "If you ever want to get out of here, you can always come and stay with me," he said. I wasn't even sure where that was—North Carolina or Ohio maybe—but I could tell he totally understood my situation, as if he had lived through it himself. I let his words calm me. I let them give me hope for some kind of escape. And though I never took advantage of his offer, I still remember those words.

Seventh Grade

I was a terrible seventh grader. I made no effort with schoolwork and rarely bathed. I was one of just four boys in concert choir, the reasons I joined still a mystery to me. Perhaps the last fragments of pop-star dreams still squirmed inside my queasy gut. One boy in choir, Mike Rome, was very mean to me. He'd point out when my hair was especially greasy or had dandruff flakes. I started to get pimples as well. My hormones had a war with my body and slaughtered it from the inside out. On the day when Ronald Reagan was shot, our class was interrupted by the announcement squawking over the intercom. Our teacher, Miss Haff, an obese woman whose body resembled one of those Weeble toys, turned on our classroom television. We watched in silence as they showed the shaky footage of John Hinckley Jr.'s attack. As the day wound down, I secretly hoped that Reagan would die. I craved a tragedy for everyone.

After the class, Miss Haff asked me if I could stay after and finish an assignment. I had no clue how to do it. She asked me why I wasn't paying attention in class. I started balling my eyes out. She tried to console me and told me I was going through puberty and that it was a tough time. She hugged me until I stopped hyperventilating. I felt covered by her. I was disgusted and then relaxed.

At the end of that school year, our choir was having buttons made for everyone as a souvenir. We could have our real names or a nickname on ours. We went around the room, each person saying what they'd like on their button. When it came to me I blurted out, "Desperado." The other kids grimaced my way and some of them giggled. Mike Rome called me Desperado for the next year, but not in a nice way.

United

As I became more insecure in seventh grade, my brother Matt was starting to make real friends in high school. He was the first black student ever to attend Kennewick High, and because of that, he was probably the first and only black person they knew. At this point in his life, Matt still didn't have a good idea who his father was and never felt like he could pry into the matter. A nagging feeling of not knowing who he was always shadowed him. Some people asked him if he was Mexican and some asked him if he was adopted. When he signed up to play on the high school football team, the coach wanted him to play running back and said he was going to make him "the team's Walter Payton." The implied stereotype of the comment weighed heavily on Matt's mind for a long time.

Besides, his favorite sport was actually hockey. But there wasn't a hockey team in Kennewick. And at the time, I don't even think there were any black players in the NHL. I remember the New York Rangers were always playing on the USA Network and that was Matt's favorite team. I'd hear him shouting and cheering from his bedroom (he was lucky enough to have a TV in his room). He really got into it. Sometimes I'd watch the Rangers with him, but I couldn't get excited about it.

I much preferred watching football with him. We would usually turn down the volume and pretend to be the play-by-play announcers. We were big fans of Howard Cosell and Brent Musburger. This was also around the time when we tape-recorded fake talk shows with fake commercials, inspired by Martin Mull's old show, *America 2-Night*.

At school, Matt mostly hung out with three guys who also felt like outsiders. Anthony was Japanese, George was Mexican, and J.D. was Ukrainian. They called themselves the United Nations.

J.D. was Matt's closest friend and they did things pretty often after school. The first time that Matt went to J.D.'s house didn't go well though. He rode his bike there after school and knocked on the door. Apparently, J.D.'s mom didn't know that her son had a black friend. She opened the door with a look of panic on her face and told Matt that he couldn't come in. "You shouldn't be friends with J.D.," she said. "If my husband finds out, he will shoot you."

Matt got on his bike and rode home in tears. J.D. heard about what had happened and confronted his parents. He told them that Matt was his friend for life and that he would not allow them to treat him like that again. After that, Matt spent a lot of time at J.D.'s house and his parents never had a bad thing to say.

Still, Matt did wonder if there was a gun in the house, and if it had ever been fired.

Monday Mornings

I was addicted to football statistics.

Every Sunday during football season I would jump up and down and yell at the television.

Then, on Monday mornings, I would sprint the two blocks to the newspaper machines at the post office. My dog, Scooter, would lope alongside me and I pretended he was a linebacker trying to tackle me. I'd always bought a *USA Today* or a *Seattle Post-Intelligencer* because they had the best stats; I'd cut them out and later add them up during my first-period class. I never liked the Seattle Seahawks because I had an unexplainable dislike for local teams. My favorite football team was the St. Louis Cardinals (who later became the Arizona Cardinals). Picking my favorite team as a kid was mostly based on who had the coolest helmet. I liked the profiled cardinal head and the dark red of their uniforms. All my friends liked the other popular teams of the seventies—the Cowboys, Steelers, and Chargers. The Cleveland Browns didn't have anything on their helmets. I couldn't fathom why anyone would like them.

As I ran back home I would imagine myself as a wiry punt returner like Terry Metcalf or a powerful running back like Ottis "OJ" Anderson. My dog was actually named

after Ottis Anderson. I had heard that Ottis had the nickname Scooter when he was younger.

The newspaper in my hand turned into a football and I
would dodge tacklers, set records, and make highlights that
would never be shown.

Tackle Football

Matt and I played football a lot growing up. Most of the time we'd play with the neighbor kids in Miss O'Hara's yard, which was about half the size of a real football field. We'd ask her first and most of the time she'd say yes, unless she had company and didn't want to hear all of our yelling. We called her yard O'Hara Stadium. We had to be careful because there was a water faucet sticking up, about groin-level, right in the middle of the field. Amazingly, we avoided any serious injuries there.

I loved playing football but played only one season in high school. I didn't like having to memorize plays and I didn't like getting hit. I was a wide receiver and I caught one pass the whole season (a screen play). I preferred the backyard style of game played with the neighborhood kids or, later on, with Matt and his friends, who were all older and much bigger than me. I'd tag along each Saturday to Underwood Park. One of Matt's friends was the older brother of a short, stocky girl named Jane who was trying to get permission to play on the high school football team. She'd play with us sometimes and she was really good, not afraid to hit and be hit (we played tackle). But one week she ran into the pole that marked the back of one of the end zones. It knocked her out and she stopped coming around after that.

My size worked to my advantage with these guys. I was speedy and elusive, the guy you'd have to watch out for on the "long bomb" route. Or I'd catch short passes and run out of bounds before I could get clobbered.

Hostages

One morning in early 1981, I was at my friend Brian's house, where I had spent the night. His family had lived just down the street from mine but was now in a much bigger house in an area where a lot of new houses were being built. Brian was a year younger than me but he always played football with Matt and me and the other neighborhood kids. He had a good arm and I always thought he'd be a star quarterback.

We were in his front yard, playing catch, when his mom came out and excitedly told us that the American hostages in Iran were going to be set free. Although I didn't understand the situations behind the hostage crisis, it was something that I thought about for a lot of that year when it was happening. As in: *What would I do if I were held hostage for 444 days?* It was a hypothetical source of worry and paranoia for me. I was starting to doubt America's power.

Brian must have been asking himself those same hypothetical questions, because we looked at each other and I could tell he was as relieved as me. We started jumping around and whooping it up. We dashed into the wide new streets of the housing development and ran along them, up and down the paved hills, shouting, "The hostages are free! The hostages are free! The hostages are free!"

CCD

From sixth to eigth grade, Dad made me go to a Wednesday-night Catholic Bible study thing called CCD (Confraternity of Christian Doctrine). It was held in a building behind the church. I have very little recollection of it, because I constantly skipped it. Instead, I would hang out at the bowling alley next door for an hour, playing video games. I was obsessed with these new machines, my favorites being Space Invaders, Battlezone, and Pac-Man. I even bought the books that showed you different play patterns to use. I prided myself on making up my own strategies though, and I was really good, topping the high score and creating calluses on my thumb at the same time.

Dad never found out that I was skipping so much. I did go to the class just enough to earn a certificate. It said I was a confirmed Catholic.

Protestant

I went to a friend's church with him when I was sixteen. It was much more exciting than the dull Catholic church that Dad and I went to. I told Dad I was thinking about switching churches, not realizing it would be a big deal.

He was not happy about this. Mark had gone to Mass with him before, when I was a baby, but somehow was able to get out of it eventually. I was the only family member who went to Mass with him. I used to wonder why Mom didn't go either, but Dad explained to me once, with a dismissive wave of his hand, that she wasn't religious. He thought I was having a spiritual crisis and made an appointment for me to see the priest, to have a talk with him at the church offices.

Dad explained to me that the church I wanted to go to was a Protestant church and that the word *Protestant* came from *protest*. "The Protestant Church is for people who protest the Catholic Church," he explained. "The Catholic Church is the original faith and Protestants were the people who left the Church."

The priest chided me lightly with a mix of pity and disappointed detachment when I visited him the next day. I looked around at the office, which was down the street from the church, and wondered if he lived there. There were alarming signs of normalcy—a television, regular clothes draped on the arm of a couch, some mystery paperbacks, a dusty refrigerator. I nodded and half-listened to his lecture, but mostly my mind wandered. I realized that the part of Mass I would miss the most was communion. For some reason that was never clear to me, I wasn't supposed to eat an hour before church started. So by the time everyone lined up for the communion wafer, I was starved and ready to consume what essentially was a snack to me. In fact, I thought it would be amazing to break into the church some night and steal a whole box of the things. I imagined myself chomping away on them as I watched TV.

The priest cracked my daydream by asking if I wanted to put my soul in danger by abandoning the church. I felt bad because I hadn't been listening close enough to what he'd been saying, so I simply said no, I didn't want to endanger my soul. I would remain a Catholic.

After church the following week, the priest shook my hand and gave me his best look of forgiveness.

Centipede

After this "lapse of faith" (as Dad called it), he acted a little more cold to me at church, sitting a couple of inches farther away and never looking my way. At one Sunday evening Mass, I suddenly started to feel warm and queasy. I was stuck between an older obese man on my right and Dad on my left. I told Dad that I needed to go to the bathroom, but he acted like he didn't hear me. It was still early in the service and one of the third-string priests was monotoning some particular passage so heavy with ancient metaphor that it made my sickness speed up my throat. I threw up a little on my pant leg and Dad looked at it and shook his head, as if to say, You'd better not do that again. The obese man on my right had his eyes closed as if he were sleeping there. I looked at Dad and hoped he would let me out. When everyone finally stood up for the main gospel, Dad looked at me and said, "You stink. Go wait outside."

I walked over to the bowling alley instead and played Centipede for twenty minutes, watching the clock carefully. A white smear of sick dried on the left leg of my black pants.

Jaynee

A year or so after the fire, we were still living in the small, windowless apartment. A ten-year-old girl named Jaynee and her mother lived in the apartment above us. I don't think she had a father and her mom was rarely seen. Whenever Dad wasn't rebuilding the old house, he was hanging out with this little girl. They'd watch TV, go for walks, and play games together; things he'd never do with my brothers or me. Matt and I were curious what the deal was. They seemed to be keeping secrets. I even remember Jaynee going to Mass with us once. We suspected Dad of being a pervert. (Even before Jaynee, we noticed how he would always stare at young girls.)

We began following them on their walks and watching them through the window curtains when they would watch TV, sitting close together on the couch. Even Mom sensed something and acted tense whenever Jaynee was around. The whole family, except Dad of course, began to secretly hate Jaynee. We'd sometimes split up with walkie-talkies and spy from the bushes or trees that lined the alleyways and ditches of our neighborhood. I don't think we were jealous of them, but on some nights we'd lie in bed and hear sounds from upstairs. We wondered what was inside her heart.

Rebuilding

This is how I learned what the word *monotony* means.

Instead of using the money from the insurance company to hire builders for the house, Dad decided to "save money" by doing it himself. What he hadn't bargained for was that it would take him much longer to get it done that way. So for four years we lived in an apartment that was too small and too ugly. Matt or Mark or I would take turns helping Dad do different things at the old house. The first few things, like smashing down walls with sledge hammers and sorting through ashen remains, were fun. But then came the boring stuff like measuring and insulating. Our big job then, as Dad's assistants, was to keep the tape measure in place, or hold the flashlight when the afternoon became night.

We'd have to do this for hours each day. If it seemed like we weren't needed, we'd ask Dad: "Can I go play next door with Darren?" And he'd say: "No, I might need you to hold the flashlight."

Each morning would become a game between my brothers and me of who could leave the apartment fastest. The last one always lost. "Say, Matt, I mean Mark, I mean Kevin, don't go planning anything today. I'll need your help over at the house."

The whole rebuilding process was slower than anybody ever thought it would be. *Help* became the most painful word for my brothers and me to hear.

Mt. Saint Helens

The day that Mt. Saint Helens blew, I thought it was Doomsday. I spent the morning in church with my dad and when we came out around noon, the sky was dark and ashen, as if the sun had disappeared. Instead of going to the church basement for doughnuts, everyone stood frozen and talked quietly on the front steps of St. Joseph's.

Someone said, "Well, it really happened."

It was probably a half hour later when I finally caught on to what was happening.

The next morning, I went out with the neighbor kids and we gathered as much ash from the sidewalks and car hoods as we could. We filled up tiny bottles that formerly held Gerber baby food. Someone said the bottles would be worth money someday.

It was spring break when this happened, and when I went back to school the next week, everyone had bottles of ash to show.

Hydroplanes

The hydroplane races that happened on the Columbia River were a big event every summer in the Tri-Cities. The population of about 100,000 swelled to 150,000 for race weekend. The scene at the actual race site was like a big wild party, with people lined up along both sides of the river—the Pasco side and all through Columbia Park on the Kennewick side. There were bleary-eyed union workers freely swigging beer, stereos cranked up loud, scantily clad headbanger girls, the smell of sweat and cocoa butter lotion, and some fistfights here and there.

I wasn't allowed to go until I was thirteen, and then only if Dad went with me. So, that year, after church got out on race day morning, we headed to the river. Not wanting to pay the steep $5 charge, Dad parked somewhere along the outskirts and showed me a dark irrigation tunnel that we could sneak through to get to Columbia Park. For a moment, it wasn't like I was with my dad at all. He wasn't a humorless, God-fearing bore, but rather a rule-breaking outlaw. I almost expected him to take off his shirt and light up a joint as we walked.

When we emerged at the other side of the tunnel—an excruciating half hour later—we pushed aside an old fence and climbed up a rocky bank to get to the park. Some people saw us come in this way, but they were either embarrassed for us or didn't care. This place, where we snuck in, was the same place the bones of the famous Kennewick Man were found a few years later.

With nowhere to sit and watch, we strolled back and forth along the river, struggling to see the race through the people cheering for the boats. It didn't matter to me though. I was busy gawking at the slumped drunks, loose bikinis, muscle cars, motorcycle gangs, and skinny, pony-tailed stoners. Dad was also transfixed, especially by the bikinis.

It was like how I imagined Mardi Gras, or a college football game would be.

That was the year the Pay 'N Pak hydroplane did a double flip and almost killed its driver. I remember the sound that came from the crowd when it happened—the collective gasp, the exhale, the sudden silence.

Vibrator

Dad gave me a vibrator once. Sort of oval-shaped. He gave it to me so I could wrap it and give it to Mom as a birthday present. Later, they kept it in a drawer by the bed. Then, shortly after, they slept in separate beds.

Nicknames

In middle school, I became really good friends with a skinny redheaded kid named Maurice. We were the kind of friends who had their own secret language. We wrote notes to each other, full of weird words, and passed them to each other between classes. We decided that our parents needed nicknames.

My mom was Fuzz because she had one of those white old lady Afros that became so popular, partly due to the influence of the TV show *The Golden Girls*. My dad was Pudlow because he was kind of scrawny and weak, even though he had these little humorous outbursts (known as spazzes back then) and tried to act all authoritative. Maurice's parents' nicknames were somewhat more random and obscure. His mom was Art for the simple fact that she made some fuss about taking up painting once. Garno was his dad's nickname, because it rhymed with Yarno, and John Yarno was a big dorky-looking offensive lineman for the Seattle Seahawks at the time. Maurice told me once that his dad's fingers would often become curled in cold weather because of some metal in his hand. He called that "doing the Garno."

Country Music Memories

1. I'm in our bathroom and Dad is listening to Hank Williams on a tinny-sounding radio, which sits on the washer. I am probably six or seven. I'm sitting atop the dryer because it's warm on my bottom. I watch him shave and he sings along with Hank, sort of yodeling-like. My brothers are outside playing football with the neighbor kids. I can't play because I have the mumps. I look just like Robert Blake, who we watch on the TV show *Baretta*. I like looking at my face in the mirror as Dad sings.

2. I am supposed to meet my parents at the big fountain in the mall. I've been hanging out with my other twelve-year-old friends at the drug store, where we shamelessly loiter and look at comic books. I have to walk through JCPenney to get to the fountain. In the stereo department I hear the Charlie Daniels Band's "The Devil Went Down to Georgia." Although I'm already late to meet my folks, I sit on the floor and listen, fascinated by the singer's fast-talking tale of deceit. I am grounded for a week.

3. Not long after Charlie Daniels became a household name, I decided to go with the crowd on a certain consensus: country music is bad. I know now that much of the country music from that era (the seventies) was actually good, but I was trying to be popular. I was into the Clash and Elvis Costello. Still, Juice Newton was becoming popular at this time and she was actually playing a concert at our high school gymnasium that I wanted to attend. She was a good-looking Daisy Duke type of lady with long Crystal Gayle–like hair. Plus her name was Juice. I sat in the upper seats and discreetly tapped my toes to her hit "Queen of Hearts."

4. One of my first jobs out of broadcasting school was doing the weekend evening shows at a Spokane country music station. There was a big *History of Country Music* book that I used for little factoids when I wanted to sound like I knew what the hell I was playing. I'd talk about how Freddy Fender was once in prison or that Eddie Rabbitt was from Brooklyn. I spoke of George Jones as if we were ancient friends. I learned that I actually liked some of the music, especially the old wild hollerin' stuff like Bob Wills and Earl Scruggs. I even took a shine to singers like Tammy Wynette and Dolly Parton, whom of course I fantasized about. I even felt an emotional tug whenever I played Glen Campbell's "Wichita Lineman," looking out the big seventh-floor window and wondering, "How is my girlfriend doing me wrong tonight?"

Confession

Dad went to confession every Saturday. He always asked me if I needed to go too. Sometimes I'd say yes, just so he didn't think I was blowing it off completely.

When I did go with him I would confess things in a very general way—I said a bad word, I had dirty thoughts, I took a dollar from my mom's purse. If I wanted to be more revealing I could have mentioned my nights of amateur graffiti, looking in my cousin's underwear drawer, and stealing from the Salvation Army store.

The confessionals had two spaces for confessors, one on each side of where the priest sat. They were dimly lit on the inside and when the priest was ready to hear your confession he would slide a little door open and make the sign of the cross. There was a thin piece of fabric in that small window separating us, but I always feared that he would figure out it was me. When he spoke through the fabric, in his best soothing tone, I could see some of the features on his long face and that fabric pulsing with his breath. Sometimes I would try to hide in the darkness or change my voice a little or pretend that I was from another town. I didn't want him to look at me during Mass the next day and think to himself, *There's that little masturbator.*

My penance was usually three Hail Marys and a couple

of Our Fathers. I didn't quite understand why there had to be so much repetition. I pictured God watching over and listening in on all the penances from all over the world. Maybe it was like counting sheep to Him, a comforting lull.

I couldn't imagine what Dad had to confess every week, but he was in the confessional for a good fifteen minutes each visit. Maybe he was being forgiven for all the terrible things I learned about him later, but at the time I imagined that he just needed someone to talk to and instead of his sins, maybe he was boring the priest with stories about his job. I was also his victim in this regard. Sometimes when we were out driving somewhere, he'd start telling me about how he worked on this road and who he worked on it with and how much it cost the state. Details that had no chance of sticking to my brain.

Sitting in the pews, penance done, I watched the short line of confessors getting smaller. The monotonous whispers of the prayers around me turned to sheep and flew to the heavens to be counted and slept on.

What I Would Think About During Mass

The football games I was missing.

The woman's hair in front of me.

Who I would have to shake hands with at the "offer each other a sign of peace" part of the service.

Should I make my dad wonder what I've done by not going to communion?

Is it a sin for minors to drink the "blood of Christ"?

Are my pants too baggy?

Is the person behind me staring at my ass?

The person's ass two rows in front of me.

I wish they had chocolate-dipped communion.

It must be embarrassing being an altar boy.

Should I really try to sing, or should I moan along with everyone else?

I wonder what kinds of donuts they'll have in the basement after the service.

Am I going to miss the halftime highlights?

Physical

"**Flip me some** shit, boy. C'mon, flip me some shit."

After the P.E. soccer game we all ran back to the locker rooms to shower. I had accidentally kicked Farrell in the knee. Two of his friends ran beside him as he taunted me. He didn't need backup though. It was widely believed since grade school that Farrell was probably the meanest and biggest kid in our grade. With only Chongo being arguably tougher.

"You think you'll be okay in the shower, boy? I wouldn't want you to slip or anything," said Farrell. His friends smiled, then he tried to trip me.

Once inside, he leaned against my locker. "I don't think you got any friends in here, do ya? Nobody'd give a shit if I flushed your fucking head down the toilet. They'd probably laugh." What frightened me most about him saying this was how he said it slowly and calmly, as if discussing what was on the lunch menu.

High Dive

I never took swim lessons when I was a kid and (though I didn't announce this fact to anyone) I was terribly afraid of any water. Perhaps it was my imagination going crazy, but it seemed to me like there was a drowning at the public pool every year. When I first started high school there was a quiet Asian kid—maybe he was even a foreign exchange student—who drowned while swimming in P.E. Some kids said that his body sat at the bottom of the deep end for a good fifteen minutes before anyone noticed.

I think the *Jaws* movies probably contributed to my fear as well. I was especially haunted by the scene where Roy Scheider scubas down to inspect a sunken boat and the bloated head of one victim suddenly appears.

Our public pool was right across the street from my high school, so we had a couple of weeks each year where we swam and played water polo during P.E. class.

We practiced diving too. Going up the ladder was the dizziest part for me. I always wanted to turn back, but there were people in the way. I had no choice but to jump. I plugged my nose and dove to the right, so that I wouldn't have to swim so far to get out. I paddled like a dog. I suppose I could have learned the breaststroke but I never wanted to put my face in the water. I thought I'd open my mouth at the wrong moment and water would flood into my throat and I'd be done for, plummeting to the bottom, my lungs exploding.

One of my friends made fun of me—"Here doggy-doggy." I'd laugh along, scared for my life. When I was out of the pool, I noticed how white my feet looked. I almost wanted to swim with my socks on. I sat in a plastic chair and draped a towel over my lower legs.

When I got older, I eventually taught myself how to swim a little better and, though I was still wary of rivers and lakes, I actually enjoyed going to swimming pools. But one day while I was at a Portland pool, I must have stepped on a small piece of glass or something. I sat down on a lawn chair and noticed blood shooting out of my right big toe like a little squirt gun. I couldn't figure out what was causing this blood fountain, but it stopped after a few minutes, only to start up again at various random times for the next few months. I went to a foot doctor and he said it was probably a tiny pebble that sometimes shifted and caused the blood to pulse out. He offered to give me a shot to numb my toe, make a small cut, and peel the skin back to see what the problem was. It almost made me sick just to hear him describe the procedure. I said no thanks and decided to see if it would fix itself. A couple of months later, whatever was in there finally came out. I was healed.

Korea

Darren and I wanted to feel the skin of the cashier at the Mayfair Market.

It was cold outside and I had just gotten two ski masks from my brother Russell, who was stationed in Korea. They were Christmas presents, and I think they had trees on them—red trees on white stitching. In black letters it said KOREA on the back. Darren and I thought ski masks were funny looking, and we knew from watching TV that only people in Antarctica or guys robbing banks wore them. I gave one to Darren and we wore them on our heads but never pulled them down over our faces.

Behind the grocery store were some doctors' offices and a pharmacy. By the pharmacy was a big generator. One afternoon, we hid the two Korean ski masks behind the generator, where nobody would find them.

That night, after the store had closed, we hung out by the telephone booths. Five minutes, then fifteen, passed. Darren took a lap around the store and looked in the windows to see what the cashier was doing. She was still there and so was a yellow Volkswagen in the parking lot.

We had no knowledge of being watched, but we were. Across the street in the dark lot of a Chevron station was a police car with its lights off.

After Darren got back to the telephone booths, we talked about the girl and made a decision. As we started back to get the masks by the generator, we saw the police lights. We told the police we were looking for a cat (we whispered this alibi to each other as they got out of their car). They wrote down our names and phone numbers and asked us to show the tread on our shoes. They told us to go home and got back in their car to watch us walk away.

When I got home I remembered the ski masks by the generator. Then I quickly tried to forget.

Braces

One of my first girlfriends had braces and thick glasses and was not thought of as pretty or even anything resembling "friend" material. In fact, even though I told some people I had a girlfriend, I made sure no one saw her. I was sixteen, she was thirteen. When I had my first car (a cheap Chevette) I'd go to her house. It was nice, and big, with a pool in the backyard. I would pick her up and we would drive around and then make out somewhere. Her breath was always unpleasant, and she had stuff on her braces like she never brushed her teeth. Still, I went out of my way to spend time with her and was jealous once when she told me about an ex-boyfriend, an eighteen-year-old who had his own apartment, where he wanted her to suck his dick once. It was a story she told me with an "I can do anything to you" tone of voice.

Another time, when her parents were gone, we were in her basement. We took our shirts off on the couch. I ran my fingers over her small chest, feeling the nipples, no bigger than pimples. We stood up and slow-danced to a radio song. I picked her up and put her on the pool table. We stared at each other. "Do you want to know something I haven't done before?" she asked. I asked her what it was. "I've never had anyone kiss me upside down," she told me. She kicked the cue ball off the table.

Hiding Places

When we were getting our house done enough to move back in, Dad asked me if I wanted to pick out a ceiling for my bedroom. We went to a home decoration place and I picked out the kind that was divided up into squares. The square tiles rested on a metal framework so it kind of looked like a checkerboard. The metal part was black and the tiles were a bumpy white texture, like on a globe where you can feel the mountains.

After getting my room all set up and living in the house for a year, I realized it was weird to have that sort of ceiling, that it was usually seen only in offices and fancy modern buildings like city hall. I stood on a chair one night and pushed on one of the tiles. It moved up and slid over. I could put my hand up there and feel a couple of feet of space. I started hiding my dirty magazines up there. It seemed perfect, and it was. Dad was a snoop and would find them if I kept them under my mattress or in a sock drawer like my friends.

Years later, after I moved out, my bedroom was converted to a sewing room for Mom. My stash was gone by then, hidden somewhere in the basement. I'd still find myself looking at the ceiling though, imagining those naked women above Mom's head as she sewed.

Troubled Girl

Whenever I went to Fruitland Park to shoot baskets, I noticed a girl sitting on the porch of a house across the street. I thought she was really cute, but couldn't tell how old she was. *The Karate Kid* was my favorite movie and I'd seen it six times in the theater. She looked a little like Elisabeth Shue—I liked the scene in that movie where she had on the tight sweater and they went to the amusement park.

She started to come over to the courtside benches when I'd show up. I was nervous as I talked to her. She told me she lived with her cousins because her parents were murdered in Chicago. Nothing ever happened with this relationship, not even a kiss. She gave me Bruce Springsteen's *Born in the U.S.A.* for Christmas. I never listened to it. We drifted apart that winter, partly because it was too cold to play basketball.

Five years later, I lived in a different town and was in my twenties. I'd visit my parents for holidays, and one time she called. I met her in a grocery store parking lot and we sat in my car. The steering wheel of my car seemed enormous, almost as if it were growing in front of me, as she confessed that she had told me lies about her family. She said she was married but had always loved me. I almost wanted to kiss her but was nervous again. She said her husband beat her up sometimes and that she had a baby boy. His name was Kevin. I thought about how long she would have to live with that.

My Friend Pat

In tenth grade, I started to embrace my weirdness a little more, thanks to one of my new friends, Pat Kennelly. He was this short kid with curly white hair and glasses. He sort of looked like an albino. He lived with his family in a pretty big house a couple of blocks from the high school. We had a couple of classes together and even though I really wanted to be popular (and Pat was like a poster boy for Not Popular), Pat cracked me up and I realized we had the same kind of weird humor. We both liked *Monty Python's Flying Circus*, the movie *Airplane!*, and Devo.

I started to hang out less with Darren and Maurice. I hung out at Pat's house a lot and spent the night there on most weekends. We stayed up late and watched *Night Flight*, an assortment of music and comedy that took over the USA Network on the weekends.

At school, we would do weird things for the sake of being weird. We'd go sit in a class that wasn't ours until the teacher would look at us, puzzled, and then ask us to leave. While walking down the hallways, we'd sometimes fall to our hands and knees and spastically crawl several feet before getting back up on our feet, our facial expressions flat and muted, as if nothing goofy was happening at all. We would get in fake fights and then run away from each other, pretending to cry. If someone from Yearbook was taking photos, we'd try to get in the picture and point at something outside of the frame, sometimes with a look of glee, sometimes with an expression of horror.

We were friends for a couple of years, but something odd started to pull us apart. I really wanted to have a girlfriend and I wanted to be cool. I wasn't sure if I could hang out with Pat Kennelly and be cool. Plus Maurice would make snide remarks about Pat and how much we were hanging out. Not that Maurice was any cooler, but sometimes it's easy to be swayed by fear, and I was afraid I would lose Maurice as a friend. We'd been friends for a long time and we sometimes talked about living with each other when we got older. I think when you're a teenager and you start making plans with your friends in regards to living together or going to a college together or hunting for Bigfoot or whatever, you really get excited. Because it's the future! And it's without your parents!

I'm sad I wasn't Pat's friend for longer. I've looked through all my high school yearbooks and I don't think he even signed any. There is one funny scrawl that takes up a half page in back of my sophomore yearbook. It doesn't have a name signed to it, but it says in part:

Kevin,

    Guilty! Where is the fish? Dance with the flame! The yellow man inside that egg is in love with Big Leggy! Vegetables!

I'm pretty sure that's from Pat.

Trespass

Once, during a snowy winter break, Maurice and I were jonesing to play basketball, so we walked over to our high school to see if any of the doors were open. Sometimes there were doors left open near the gym because there were teams practicing or a janitor working.

We got there and found the doors unlocked and the gym lights on, but no one else around. No sign of a janitor. We had our boom box with us and plugged it in at court-side. We had some sodas and a bag of chips from the store. It was like we had set up camp for the night.

We shot baskets on the beautiful hardwood floors and listened to Kurtis Blow and the Bar-Kays. About an hour into our private practice, three cops appeared. Two of them were up in the stands, walking around as if we had hidden bombs somewhere, and one of them approached us on the court. "What are you guys doing here?" he asked. Maurice turned the music down and told him we were just shooting baskets and that the doors were open and that we were students of the high school. They took our names and phone numbers and made us walk back home in the snow.

When school started again in January, we were called into the office and told we were to do Saturday school for two weeks because of our "trespassing." The school narc gave us each a police report and told us to have our parents sign them. Maurice and I went home that day, nervous that they had called our parents. They hadn't, so we forged the signatures on the reports and served our two weeks of Saturday school without our parents knowing.

Big Gulp

For most of my junior year of high school, I developed a strange dietary ritual. Before school, I would start my day with a package of Hostess Donettes (usually the waxy chocolate-covered ones) and a Big Gulp of Pepsi. Once at school, I'd put the Big Gulp in my locker and use it for quenching my thirst throughout the day, even past the point when the melted ice took over the cola flavor. My locker partner ridiculed me.

It was almost like an eating disorder. I put inexplicable pressure on myself to finish the drink before my last class of the day. I threw up a couple of times.

If I wasn't eating Donettes for breakfast, then cereal was the usual replacement. I was a very picky eater. If I woke up early enough, I took a couple of pieces of my dad's bacon. For dinner, we had very typical meat and potato kind of meals. We rarely ate out but when we did it was usually at Skipper's on Friday nights or, on rare occasions, if the parents were feeling flush, Sizzler. At the end of these meals, Dad, too embarrassed to ask for a doggy bag, would wrap his leftovers in napkins and stick them in his pockets.

Suitcase

When I was fifteen years old, I had a suitcase full of porn. It was greenish blue—the aged color of flat turquoise. Square and heavy. Two metal latches kept it shut. Two buttons popped the latches. I kept it in the back of the closet, behind the clothes, and next to another suitcase that didn't match. We were a poor family without nice things.

The suitcase, for me in the eighties, served as a "best of" fantasy portal. Whereas now, most adults—and yes, even fifteen-year-olds—keep their "best of" porn in a folder on their computer. Who needs all that paper anyway? I could do without all the wordiness of *Playboy* and *Penthouse*. I wanted skin. Photos. Pictures. Images to fill my eyes and mind. So two things happened—I started to find magazines that were almost entirely photos, and because I was accumulating too many magazines to hide, I started to cut out just my favorite images. It was like clipping coupons.

I had various ways to get these magazines. I had friends with cars and the knowledge of a specific Dumpster. I had an older brother who had his own place. I had a cousin who hid porn in the closet. Those were my sources.

The cousin was the most interesting. She was young and married. Her husband had a mustache and drove one of those Snap-on tools trucks around (I'm not sure why that seems significant, but it does). When I was younger, even before puberty, I remember wanting to kiss her knees, to touch her legs. But my incestuous urges were pushed aside by childish angst whenever she talked to me in condescending baby talk. So it was most satisfying when I found her "marital aides." Not only was there a box of magazines and erotica books (bedtime reading, I presume), there were also films. Not videos, but actual plug-in-the-projector-and-loop-it-to-a-reel films. This was on a night when she and her husband were out and Matt and I were having a sleepover at their house. We found the projector and tried nervously to snake the film through it. We found a blank wall to shine our jittery smut on. The grainy color film was upside down or backward or maybe both. It was confusing but it was the first moving sex pictures I'd seen. We put everything back before they got home, but I managed to slip two magazines—smaller, *Reader's Digest*–size ones with foreign words on the cover—into my sleeping bag.

Later, at home, behind the locked door of my bedroom, I looked through one of them and tried to follow a story just by the photos. The language was strange, maybe French. I couldn't make out anything. But the images gave me an idea: A young man working at a grocery store helps a woman out with her shopping cart. She has poufed-out red hair and wears a short skirt. Her legs look smooth and strong. She also wears a loose blouse that looks slack and thin over her cleavage. As the boy starts putting the bags of groceries in the back of her minivan, she climbs in the back and feigns to help him, making room and crawling on her knees in front of his face. He reaches up her leg and she looks back at him and smiles. He glances around the parking lot before climbing into the van. Her clothes come off quickly and he eagerly covers her from behind, his pants around his ankles. I put my own translation into the captions around the photos. I think the woman probably talked to him as he touched her but I couldn't fathom what she might be saying. Maybe it was just heavy breathing. Heavy breathing is the same in every language. When I cut those photos out of the magazine, I kept some of the mysterious language in there. It was a reminder of something I couldn't explain. I used those pictures, that story, over and over, for my own foreign pleasure.

Pee-Chees

Before the suitcase, there were Pee-Chees, folders usually reserved for keeping schoolwork in. Illustrated with images of football players, track runners, baseball hitters, and pom-pommed cheerleaders, I filled them with my favorite clippings of naked women. This was also done because of space issues. With magazines, sometimes I'd have to find more than one image to look at. I'd spread open magazines all across my bed, but that seemed so arduous. One fateful afternoon, I snagged some scissors from my mom (she often sewed in the room next to mine). I waited for everyone to leave the house and then proceeded to scavenge through the stack of magazines. I'd been keeping my stash in the ceiling of my room. It had those big suspended tiles and all I had to do was stand on a chair and push one of them aside to sneak stuff in and out. But I was getting worried about the weight and girth of my porn. It actually took me a few days to go through it all with the scissors. I had to determine which images turned me on and which ones didn't. I found that I wanted a little of everything: big breasts, small breasts, skinny, chubby, blond, brunette, black, white, Asian, purple, short hair, long hair, big bushy hair, glossy red lipstick, clown makeup. It turned out that I wasn't too discerning. Of course, I was also a virgin.

These Pee-Chees replaced the magazines in my ceiling. I took a Hefty garbage bag full of discarded magazine scraps and walked them over to the Mayfair Market's Dumpster after dark. I was filled with a sense of relief, like a drunk coming out of detox. I could sleep at night now, knowing that fifty pounds of dirty magazines weren't going to break through the tiles above me and pummel my face. I was comforted with the thought that only "the best" was up there. Nestled together in their Pee-Chees. Three of them. Overflowing with women reclining, leaning, jumping, pouting, posing, and playing. Sometimes I could just stare at the ceiling and I'd get hard. My focus and concentration were impressive. Above the Pee-Chees was nothing else. No roof. No sky. No God.

But I couldn't stop it there. I couldn't quit going to the porn Dumpster. Or stealing *Playboy* and *Penthouse* from the Mayfair. What I really wanted was a girlfriend, someone who would welcome my smothering affection, but I was nervous, insecure, and acne-ridden. I remember my friends who somehow attached themselves to girls and learned their rules and protocol. I tagged along with them to the park sometimes and they'd make out inside the play structure or smoke cigarettes. I waited on the swings, making myself sick. I saw Beth stick her hand down Scott's pants. It looked like she was punching him. When she took her hand away, it looked so small. Her fingernail polish was dull and sloppy. I was so horny I don't even think I could bear to hold hands with a girl.

As my Pee-Chees swelled further that year, I began to worry about my ceiling again. I didn't want it to start sagging, so I found the old turquoise suitcase and piled my stash inside. I imagined what it would be like to dress up in a suit and walk around with the suitcase like a businessman. I wanted to paint it black so it seemed less suspicious. The color was odd and kind of garish, like it was announcing itself as a vessel of smut. Even the old 1950s shape of the thing seemed pervy. My family never went on vacations or trips though, so it was a safe and unassuming place.

Joan Jett

I bought the Joan Jett cassette called *Album* (I admit I had a crush on her even though I was also scared of her). I listened to it a few times in my room, rocking out on my mushroom chair. At the end of side two was a secret unlisted song that had a chorus where Joan sang the lyrics "You're a star fucker star fucker star fucker" over and over. There was also a part about a clean pussy and giving head to Steve McQueen, but I didn't really latch on to those.

Dad charged into my room while I was listening to it and told me to turn it off. Then he ejected the cassette, pulled a bunch of the tape out, and put it on the ground. He lifted his foot high and then stepped on it. He took the cassette box from my hand and looked at the yellow cover art of Joan jumping in the air with her guitar. He said through gritted teeth, "I should just burn this crap."

I didn't know how to respond, so I just said, "Sorry."

"I don't care for any of this stuff that you listen to," he said.

He ground his heel into the plastic cassette and into the carpet. The ribbon of the tape surrounded his foot like dead baby snakes.

Dunk Contests

When we were in high school, Maurice and I would sometimes go to my old elementary school and play basketball on its court. We liked it because the hoops were made for little kids and were only eight feet tall. We mimicked our favorite dunkers (Dominique Wilkins, Julius Erving) and had dunk contests. I liked how the nets were made of chain. Each jump shot, each jam, sounded like a slot machine paying out. Once I dunked so hard that the metal backboard lost its screws and crashed to the ground. Those were good times, sweaty and dreamlike.

We played a lot of playground basketball during that time and we started a rivalry with Jeff Jones and Tim Sanders, two of the stars from our school basketball team. We beat them in a game of 2-on-2 once.

I found a book called *The In-Your-Face Basketball Book*, which was all about playground basketball. It had a section where they talked about all the good courts to play on around the country. Instead of hunting for Bigfoot, I started to dream of this adventure instead. Pulling off the highways to play pickup games in every state, the sun casting our darting shadows. We played until the ball got too slick and then we cooled down with a Slurpee or a Big Gulp.

The one thing I didn't like about Maurice at the time

was that he was a Lakers fan. My favorite team was the
76ers and I suffered through many postseason heartbreaks
around that time. Their championship season in 1983
made up for all of that though. They swept the Lakers in
the finals and to celebrate, Mom took me to Burger King.

Echo

Maurice and I found a pile of discarded basketball jerseys at a sporting goods store on Clearwater Avenue. We assumed they were from some small town school that we had never heard of—perhaps a school from Moses Lake or Wenatchee. They said ECHO on the front, with the number underneath. We found the numbers that we thought were the coolest (he was 8, I was 21).

As we rode the bus home (public transportation was new in the Tri-Cities at the time), we decided that we needed a story to go with our new jerseys. Instead of saying "Echo," we would say it was pronounced "Ee-cho." It was decided that this was not the name of a school, but rather the name of another planet. A planet that we were from, and a planet where everyone wore Converse shoes, because we had a stout devotion to Chuck Taylors. We thought our enemy planet should be Lovetron, a fictional planet that backboard-shattering basketball star Darryl Dawkins often talked about. On Lovetron, everyone wore Nikes. We refused to wear Nikes. In fact, to this day, I have never worn Nikes.

We called ourselves the Duo of Doom.

Licorice

Maurice and I hung out at this record store in Pasco called the Licorice Donut. We used to buy all our records there. This was when we were really into funk. During the school year we'd even go home for lunch just to watch *Video Soul* on the BET (Black Entertainment Television) station.

Every time we went to the Licorice Donut we'd buy something different. We bought our first hip-hop records there (Kurtis Blow, Grandmaster Flash, various Sugar Hill and Def Jam releases) and later we'd have him special order punk rock for us too.

Maurice and I took a Radio/TV class our junior and senior years of high school. It was at the Vocational Center, where kids from other high schools also came to take specialty classes. Our class had a production room where we would record our own raps using the B-side instrumentals. We were supposed to be taping promo spots for the student station. We hung out with these two black kids from Pasco High named Richie Rap and Ronnie Rhyme. Richie dressed like 1984-era Michael Jackson with the red multizippered jacket and black parachute pants (also zippered more than needed) and he always had girls after him because of that. He did well in that regard. He had a nice personality and his rap style was probably the smoothest of all of us. Ronnie was a more awkward guy. He looked too old to be in school and had a slouch. He made the most mistakes with his raps, getting off rhythm, flubbing words, and stepping on others' lines. We managed to record three or four songs during junior year.

That summer, Maurice and I got a job spinning records at a bowling alley where they had a weekly break-dancing contest. It was strange how being a DJ made it easier to talk to girls. My habit of mixing in New Wave songs with hip-hop eventually cost us the job.

Lionel Live

In 1984, my brother Mark drove Maurice and I across the state to see Lionel Richie at the Tacoma Dome. We had an extra ticket so he went to the show with us, even though he was a stoner and preferred Blue Öyster Cult. Tina Turner opened for him, but it was just before her big comeback and I didn't really care about her. Even though I had seen a couple of bands in smaller settings, I still consider this my "first big concert."

About halfway through Lionel's awesome set, it looked like Mark was about to cry. He was singing along, cheering, and shouting "We love you, Lionel!" between the songs. When Lionel played the old Commodores tune "Brick House" my brother danced the funky chicken. It was like witnessing a religious awakening.

When we got back to Kennewick, Mark wore his Lionel Richie T-shirt unflinchingly. Maybe it was the power of pot, but I'd like to think it was the power of soul.

Big Momma's

My first job after I turned sixteen was at a family-run pasta place called Big Momma's. I was hired as a dishwasher/busboy but was promoted to waiter within a week after the waitress quit. There was a small dining room with a bar in the back. Most of the time it was just the bartender, the cook, and me. On the busy nights, I got some help from Tonya, the owner's daughter, who was a year older than me and had the biggest breasts I've ever seen on a teenager. But she was really bossy and spoiled and I enjoyed seeing her more when she wasn't in the kitchen yelling at someone.

There was also a really nice waitress named Deanna who was nineteen and treated everyone like she was their mom. She was going out with Jim, the main cook. Jim was tall and wiry, with shaggy hair, a big nose, and a perpetual five o'clock shadow. He must have been ten or twenty years older than Deanna. We had a cassette player in the kitchen and we took turns playing music on it. I would bring in tapes by groups like Cameo and Midnight Star and Jim would play Judas Priest or, oddly enough, James Taylor.

Jim and Deanna were a good couple though, and they lived together in a cluttered apartment close to my high school. They invited me over to their place a few times and Deanna even set me up on a blind date with one of her friends. The friend was cute, like Valerie Bertinelli, and I was thrilled when we chose to go to a haunted house. That meant my date would probably get scared and grab my arm or even hold my hand. Of course, that's exactly what happened, but I probably blew any chances with her when I tried to kiss her later in the 7-Eleven parking lot.

One of my favorite people at Big Momma's was Joan, a frizzy-haired bartender who would sneak into the kitchen several times each night and fish the biggest chunk of Roquefort out of the blue cheese dressing. I thought it was gross at first, mainly put off by the stink, but I learned to love it soon enough. Each night I worked with Joan turned into a blue cheese fishing battle.

By the summer of 1985, after I had graduated high school, I was dressing a little more strangely than most Tri-Citians. I would wear double-breasted dress jackets that Mom sewed for me, combined with stretch pants, Beatle boots, earrings, and shiny broaches. The boss eventually called me to the back and hinted that I was going too far, and without giving me a second chance, they fired me. When I got home that night, I tried to feel good about not having a job but I ended up on Mom's lap, embarrassed and crying.

Cruising

I wouldn't say I had a prostitute obsession, but when I was sixteen—just old enough to drive my Chevy Malibu—Maurice and I would cruise around east Pasco, looking at any cheap hooker the streets had to offer. We did so in silence, an unspoken pull toward what our small town had deemed "the ghetto." The first few times we trolled this area, we just looked around, our imaginations coloring in details about every abandoned building and the discarded pieces of torn clothing that littered the cracked sidewalks in front of them. We eventually got comfortable enough to wonder aloud about how much the women charged for their services. We'd pull over and ask them sometimes, careful to strike some sort of balance between business-like firmness and nonthreatening friendliness. The girls humored us, talking dirty and sometimes letting us touch their breasts. We must have looked out of place on those streets, two puberty-wracked white boys—me with my pimples and braces, Maurice with his red hair and freckles. Both of us were still reluctant virgins posing as street-smart kids.

There was one thrilling night when we actually let two of the girls in my car. They wanted a ride to a hotel that was on the other side of the tunnel that separated Pasco from east

Pasco. Maurice and I listened in on their conversation during the ten-minute drive. They talked about clothes, cigarettes, and carrying guns. When we let them out, they walked to our windows and kissed us like we were their pimps.

This was around the time I started working at Big Momma's, where I made anywhere from ten to thirty dollars a night in tips, which I carelessly spent at the record store. I hadn't had a girlfriend yet—in fact, I had barely kissed a girl. But I was eager to have sex and had, coincidentally, been training for such an event for at least two years, masturbating regularly with my mom's back-rubbing vibrator, timing the seconds it took for me to ejaculate, like some perverted scientist.

I had no prospects for girlfriends. I was shy and anxious and probably a little gross. But the prostitutes were hardly out of my league. Most were not pretty at all and actually rather unhealthy looking. If they were better looking, they probably would have been working in Seattle or Portland or even Spokane. That's what I came to reason. Still, they were women who had sex a lot and, I imagined, could show me a thing or two. I wasn't picky. I was desperate.

My sexual yearning came in two dominant fantasies: One was romantic love. I listened to sappy love songs by the likes of Lionel Richie, Peabo Bryson, and Luther Vandross and I cried my eyes out, wondering if I could ever experience the depth of love in their music. When they sang about happiness or heartbreak, I felt that happiness or heartbreak, minus the actual presence of a female. The other fantasy was simply fucking. As in, fucking anything that moved. Humping, screwing, boning. You get the picture.

I began forsaking Maurice and going out by myself. He was my only real hanging-out friend at the time, so it was hard to pull off sometimes. I'd get off work and call him to tell him I was just going home or had to work late. It felt a little like I was cheating on him.

One night I decided I'd had enough of my virginity. I hit the gloomy streets of Pasco, my Malibu crawling at a steady twenty miles per hour. There was no one out. I stopped at a taco stand and ate something disgusting, killing more time and shaking with nerves. That's when I saw her, coming around a corner a block away. I jumped back in the car and drove over. For some reason, I couldn't just walk down there. I had to have something to hide behind, a getaway. The car would make me feel like I was somewhat guarded and safe.

As I got closer to her, I realized I didn't have a choice. She was the one. I wasn't going to wait any longer. I rolled my window down and asked her the question. She gave me a couple of options, like a menu or a list of the nightly specials. Fifteen dollars for a hand job, twenty-five for straight sex, and fifty bucks for a suck and fuck. Apparently, it was a bargain night. I told her I wanted what she called "straight sex," which sounded like a good introduction for a beginner like me. She got in my car and gave me directions to a motel. She was probably in her midtwenties, short and a little chubby. Her dark hair was styled unattractively and she looked bored. If this were a girl I saw at a school dance I wouldn't have looked at her twice. Her name was Greta.

When we got to the motel, she opened the door to her room and went immediately to the bathroom. She told me to take out the money and get undressed. I took off all my clothes except my boxers and socks. She came out of the bathroom, wearing a bathrobe, and walked to the bed. She gave me a condom and told me I had to put it on. She lay on the bed and opened her robe, letting it stay under her like a beach towel. Her body was unfit and slack. More like a trucker's body than a prostitute's. I didn't feel any hot sexual vibe from her at all, more like a "Can I smoke my Marlboro yet?" kind of vibe. I started to have second thoughts and wanted to renegotiate the price. I told her I was nervous because it was my first time, maybe hoping for some sort of discount. Her demeanor softened a little and she started cooing warm sentiments to me as she touched my penis with her hand to make me hard. I struggled with the condom, afraid I'd lose my erection if I didn't get it on fast enough. I had experimented with a condom just days before, putting one on and jacking off with it. My hand smelled bad for the rest of the day, but I couldn't help instinctively sniffing my fingers when no one was looking.

I got on the bed and fell on top of her. I could barely feel myself inside her. I wasn't really certain I *was* inside her. I wasn't sure what to do with my hands or if I was allowed to kiss her. I didn't know if I wanted to kiss her. I touched her breasts, they seemed saggy, unloved, the huge dark areolas looking like sad raccoon eyes. She said something strange to me, like, "It's going to be all right" or "Move down a little." I can't really remember what was said but it was very little. As I tried to get into a comfortable position, a position where I could feel something, I noticed that she was looking over my shoulder. I heard the hum of a muted television. It was mounted, hospital-style, near the ceiling. She was watching something on TV while I tried to make her come alive. I kissed her neck and her shoulders to see if I could regain her attention, but she stayed focused on the screen. I still wasn't sure if I was inside her. All I felt was air. I moved my hips carefully, so I wouldn't cum before I even felt her. But I was already getting to that point. If she would have grunted once I'm sure I would have lost it in a second. I tried to focus on the fact that she was a woman and we were naked and she was underneath me in a bed and that this was what I had seen in dirty magazines and in late-night fuzzy pay-channel movies. For a moment, I removed myself from what was happening and tried to imagine what it looked like in a magazine or on a screen. Greta, this naked woman I was trying to have sex with, was still watching the TV above us. I compromised in my mind and imagined that she was watching us having sex. That thought was enough to get me thrusting. I ejaculated quickly and unceremoniously. I tried to keep going but she asked me if I was done. I got out of the bed and thanked her.

As we left the motel, I felt embarrassed and gypped. She asked if I could drop her off at her corner. As we drove I thought she might say something about doing it again sometime, but she didn't. She simply got out at her corner and slammed the door.

I drove home that night, not feeling changed at all, like I thought I might. I wasn't about to tell Maurice about Greta and I didn't feel like driving around those dark streets with him ever again.

Late Movies

After we got our first VCR, I started using it to record my favorite videos off MTV. VH1 had started during my last year of high school as well, but they mostly played boring adult contemporary music. I would spend hours watching music videos with the VCR remote in my hand, ready to record whenever something cool came on. Videos were so fresh and fascinating at the time. The pop star dreams I had as a little kid were even bigger as an MTV-watching teenager. When no one else was around, I'd watch some of these compilation videotapes that I made. I'd work the pause button with great skill while watching videos by Madonna, Lisa Lisa and Cult Jam, and Robert Palmer. Eventually, I got a membership at the nearby video store and started watching movies on the VCR. Maurice or Darren or some other friend would spend the night and we'd be watching a movie in the front room of the rebuilt house. Sometimes, late at night, Dad would come out wearing long johns and a ratty T-shirt. He would do two things: he would tell us to turn down the volume and then he'd say, "This isn't one of those rated-R movies, is it?"

Pam

By the time I was eighteen, I had my first real girlfriend. One who would kiss me in front of people and tell me about her periods. It took two months for Pam and me to have sex. She wasn't a virgin like me. (Okay, I wasn't technically a virgin either, but did my first time really count? Emotionally I still felt like a big virgin.) She lost her cherry, she told me, when she was fifteen, to a nineteen-year-old who used to babysit her. I didn't know what a "cherry" was exactly, but her announcement gave me a stomachache. One of the dirty magazines I sought out heavily at that time was called *Cheri*. It was sleazier than most of the others. In one pictorial, a group of women took turns on a giant chocolate dildo to see who was the blow job queen.

Some of the other magazines I grew bored of. I had heard cautionary tales about porn being like a drug. That I would start to need harder, stronger, more dangerous forms of pornography. A few years later, Ted Bundy mentioned having this problem. Many people thought he was trying to blame pornography for his sick crimes, and I constantly wondered if something was wrong with me as well.

The day after I lost my virginity with Pam, I thought I could get rid of the suitcase. I thought I would want the real thing from there on out. Not only could I have sex with Pam but I could play my Commodores albums for her and she would write me love notes with big bubble letters and heart-shaped happy faces with wide-open hug arms and Flintstone feet. I thought I'd be happy.

We met each other at the Vocational Center where I was taking the Radio/TV class. She was taking some kind of retail class where the students ran a small deli-style store for all the students in the building. I'd go in there and buy Skittles and we'd pass notes to each other. If I didn't go to the store during each break she would think I was mad at her and she would write a note and have someone give it to me. She was both insecure and bossy. She went to Kamiakin, which was the rival high school in Kennewick.

For most of that senior year, I left the suitcase to fester in the closet. It just sat there, barricaded by the shirts and *Miami Vice*–style jackets my mom made for me with her constantly running sewing machine. I thought that Pam would somehow notice a difference if I masturbated during this time. I thought it would be cheating.

Right before graduation, I went to Pam's place to surprise her. It was down a long, unlit, winding road in the desert terrain behind the Columbia Center Mall. She lived in a trailer kind of thing. A big, flat rectangle of a structure with a couple of tires on the roof for some reason. She wasn't there, so I sat on her front porch talking to her younger sister for a long time until a fancy old Mustang pulled into the big lot in front of their house. This car sat idling in the dark for a few minutes. The windows were tinted. The engine finally turned off. It was the old babysitter boyfriend, Pam's sister told me. He was in town visiting.

Maybe he saw me sitting up there, waiting. Maybe they thought of pulling out, going somewhere else. Or maybe they didn't care. It seemed like a long time and I wondered what was happening in that car. My thoughts ran wild and my gut clenched. Pam's sister knew something bad was happening and she went inside so I could figure out how to "handle it."

Finally the Mustang started again and Pam stepped out. The car rolled through the loud gravel before getting back on that twisting road. I walked down from the porch to meet Pam, but she pushed me away and went inside.

The next day, I called her and listened as she described to me what had happened. I felt hollowed out and light-headed. I pulled the suitcase out of the closet and locked my door as I heard her tell her side of things. I wanted to interrupt her and tell her about the suitcase, to make her jealous of the photos and how much I liked them. About how fantasy was sometimes better than reality, which was how I wanted to feel when the heartache went away.

Sixty-three Times

I went out with Pam for about nine months. She was the kind of girl who still slept with oversize teddy bears, wrote in huge loopy cursive, and whose favorite food was pancakes. I often went to her house after school and we'd make out in her room. She lived with her mom, who had a British accent for some reason, and didn't seem to mind if Pam locked her bedroom door while I was there. Her younger sister lived there too, and she was much more attractive than Pam.

After we had sex for the first time, I went to school the next day feeling like a new person—the excitement of the sex, and the promise of more sex to come, made me feel like I was neon-lit from the inside.

On the back of Pam's school photo (her hair parted in the middle and wind-swept back, her baby blue sweater with the shoulder pads, her ill-fitting blue jeans) I took a pen and drew a mark. A few days after that, another mark. I'm not sure why, but I felt the need to document, to count, the times we did it. I never told Pam I was keeping track. Perhaps I thought I was going to keep track forever, with every girlfriend, every crash-and-burn monthlong failure, every one-night stand. When other people talked about how many people they'd had sex with, I could tell them exactly how many *times* I'd had it.

Once when I was at the mall with Pam, we were paying for food at Orange Julius when her photo fell out of my Velcro wallet. She noticed the marks and asked me what they were and I told her it was the number of records I'd bought that year. Cassettes and records, I had to tell her.

At some point, I told a friend of mine about the count. Since none of my friends liked Pam, it was only a matter of time before this friend told a few others. To embarrass me at any time they'd ask, "How many times has it been now?"

When my relationship with Pam ended bitterly, the count was over. The final number was sixty-three. Eventually, after I started seeing other girls, I felt disgusted by the number. Sometimes, just to put me in my place, a friend of mine would still smile and laugh and say to me, "Sixty-three times."

Vodka and Squirt

Even though I seemed immune to pot, I found other ways to alter my consciousness. It took a while though, as I had to get over the ingrained fears of brain damage and eternal damnation from a Catholic God. Sobriety was something I took pride in as a teen. There were other kids in high school who were infamous drunkards and potheads, but I kept a safe distance from them.

The first time I gave in to drink was a couple of nights before my high school graduation. I went over to Deanna and Jim's apartment after work.

Their place had that uncomfortable decor that happens when an older guy hooks up with a younger girl. Teddy bears and angel imagery mingled with mirrors that had whiskey logos on them. High school yearbooks from the early seventies sitting next to ones from the mid-eighties.

That night we sat in beanbag chairs and drank sweet mixed drinks (like cheap vodka and Squirt) through straws. Jim started telling really crude sexual jokes and I could tell it was making Deanna really uncomfortable. But the more I drank, the more I laughed along with Jim. I drank myself into a spinning night of sleep on their couch and woke up with a furry blanket on top of me. I was hot and felt sick. I looked at the clock and saw that I was late for my graduation rehearsal. I got up and slumped outside.

I looked around for my car and then realized I had left it at Big Momma's. I had to walk about twenty blocks to my high school. My hangover made me not care so much about being late for the rehearsal. Maurice was probably the only one who would notice I wasn't there anyway. The heat was getting to me and I did that thing with my T-shirt where you pull the front up over your head but keep the sleeves around your arms. Suddenly I felt the sickness come up and I heaved the sour throw-up next to a tree in someone's front yard. I wiped my mouth with a leaf and kept walking in the direction of my school. I started to feel self-conscious, speed walking with my shirt up like that, my face melting like a sick drunk's. People were driving by me on Garfield Avenue, probably wondering why I wasn't at school. A couple of blocks later, my legs buckled. I rested on one knee and quickly vomited between a STOP sign and a storm drain. Before I reached the school, there was one more retching moment between cars in a church parking lot.

Maurice looked at me harshly when I finally got there toward the end of rehearsal. He could somehow tell that I'd been drinking, but instead of lecturing me he said that he too was going out to get drunk that night. I wasn't sure if this was some kind of reverse psychology on his part. Maybe he was jealous because I didn't get drunk with him. Nonetheless, it made our graduation night stressful. Maurice was probably my only true friend in my class and now there was tension.

On graduation night, there was a big Las Vegas–themed

party in the high school gym for us, the triumphant Class of 1985. Maurice told me later that it was really fun and it lasted until three in the morning. I went home immediately after throwing my graduation cap into the air. I locked myself in my bedroom and listened to music on my headphones, wondering what to do next. My mind was blank.

Homemade Clothes

One day I wore an especially effeminate shirt that Mom had made for me. Dad saw it and freaked out. It didn't help that I had recently pierced both my ears (by myself, using the potato method*) and constantly ratted my bangs too. "Why don't you just go ahead and turn him into a girl?" Dad said. Some of my guy friends I hung out with were worse. A couple of them actually did wear skirts.

At the time, I was really into paisley. Mom made me dress jackets that looked like they came from Prince's wardrobe if he were on the show *Miami Vice*. Some of my friends even asked me if she could make jackets for them. It was like I had my own personal designer. (Red Carpet Reporter: Who are you wearing? Me: This is from the Mom collection.) I loved Mom for that.

One time my friend John, who was fairly normal looking compared to the rest of our friends, was over at our house. When he left, Dad shook his head sadly and said something about John wearing mascara. But John didn't wear mascara. He just had pretty eyes.

*Potato method of ear piercing: Sterilize sharp needle. Numb earlobe with ice. Press piece of raw potato behind earlobe for support. Aim needle. Push.

The Palace

That summer, after graduation, I started to hang out at
this place called the Bingo Palace. A couple of my friends
actually worked there, calling out numbers and letters to
the weeknight gatherings of oldsters. I thought it was a cool
job and I was a little jealous. But the coolest thing about
the Palace was the Friday night all-ages dances. After the
brutal breakup with Pam, I decided that I had had enough
self-pity and disgust. I was finally feeling confident about
who I was, and besides that, it was a good place to show off
my fashion sense.

About a hundred or more pimply minors would go there
every week, and it wasn't just Kennewick kids. You'd see
the Richland punkers and preppies and the Pasco jocks and
break-dancers hanging out too. The dance floor used to be
a skating rink, so it was pretty big. Around the perimeter of
that was a carpeted area with four big mushroom-shaped
seats where each clique claimed their space. The far back
corner was where all the New Wave kids hung out, stuffing their trench coats under the mushroom and filling the
air with clove smoke. Since the different cliques of people
didn't mingle, there were never any fights. But many of the
jocks and a lot of the Wavers were weekly regulars and they
would sometimes exchange dirty looks or sarcastic com-

ments. The DJ would have to play a wide mix of music to please everyone there. Whenever songs by Love and Rockets or ABC came on, the floor would belong to the Wavers. Then Def Leppard would signal the return of the jocks and everyone else. Sometimes the DJ would slip in Anita Baker or that love song from *Footloose* and the floor would fill with anxious and nervous slow dancers.

The Friday night dances became the highlight of my week. I met many of my longtime friends at the Palace that year and I discovered a love for dancing. I even thought to myself: Dancing is my life! I live to dance! Maybe dressing up and dancing to my favorite songs was as close as I would come to being a pop star, so I went for it, and I felt euphoric afterward. I was starting to really feel myself physically in the world, self-conscious in a good way. Living in the moments of music. I remember being at the Palace and thinking about how sad it would have been to be somewhere else. All those people at home. All the people at work. Anyone, anywhere else but here—I felt sorry for them.

Water Softeners

I didn't have a job for a couple of months and I was starting to run out of money. I had a pretty large collection of
records (in milk crates) and cassettes (in fruit boxes) and I
felt a voracious need to buy music. A friend gave me a tip
on a job where all you had to do was call people on the
phone. I didn't realize at the time how painfully monotonous it was going to be.

I was cold-calling people from a photocopied list, trying
to sell them some kind of water softener system. I wasn't
even sure what it did but I was assured that it made taking a
shower feel like wet heaven.

A couple of weeks into the job, I called in to take a
night off. Instead of just faking a sickness, I told them that
my dad had a stroke. They called my house the next day
and found out it wasn't true.

Neon Vomit

My new friend Terry and I were goofing around one day and I showed him some poetry that I'd been writing. But I never called it poetry back then. They were simply called "pieces." I had seen Henry Rollins do some of his spoken word on a TV show called *IRS Records' The Cutting Edge*. He read "Family Man" and I thought it was the most hilariously uncomfortable thing ever. That was the sort of prototype I was working with. Terry liked these pieces of mine and so we decided we would turn them into songs and record them.

Our first "album" of punk rock songs was recorded on a cassette player in his bedroom and bathroom. Just Terry and me. We decided to call ourselves Neon Vomit. He was good at creating some heavy riffs based on my smallest suggestions (usually just me saying, Can you do something like this—and then imitating a guitar part with my clenched mouth), and then I would yell the lyrics in my best Rollins imitation. There were no drums, but sometimes we would bang on the toilet seat for percussion. Among the first songs we recorded was a sarcastic putdown of Doug, one of the more snooty guys in our little circle of community college New Wavers. It was called "Gee, Doug, You're So Funny" (chorus: "Gee, Doug, you're so funny / You make me want to vomit!"). Terry and I made a few tapes and passed them around the campus of Columbia Basin College and it was soon the center of a rivalry as heated as West Coast versus East Coast hip-hop.

In a classic double-cross moment, Doug somehow talked Terry into playing guitar for him on a song that he wrote called "Kevin, You're Such a Fag." I admit that it was a pretty catchy song, especially with the cool drum machine they must have borrowed from someone.

Even though it was fun to record the Neon Vomit songs, I still wanted to sing (not just yell) in a band that would actually play shows. My friend Len played keyboards and wanted to form a more traditional New Wave band—with expensive haircuts, high-fashion clothes, poetic lyrics, and a sexy name.

I was writing more and more songs as Len tried to find a guitarist and a drummer. My lyrics started to sound a little less like Henry Rollins and more like a Prince protégé. It was an embarrassing mix of those two influences, with some Cure and Scritti Politti blended in. A classic case of some journals I should have burned a long time ago. Thankfully, nothing ever came of it.

Daphne

I met Daphne at the Palace. She lived in Hermiston, so instead of driving back that night, she and a friend stayed at a cheap roadside motel. I went to the hotel too, and Daphne and I had sex on the floor while her friend slept in the bed. I liked her immediately because she also liked Prince and she was easy, like me. Easy and eager.

We saw each other off and on for a few months, whenever she came to town for the weekend dances or to shop at the mall. An alternating gaggle of other kids from Hermiston also would come up with her. They always stood out a little because their sense of style was actually more small-town than the Tri-Cities. They tried a little harder to seem different. But under their Goth makeup and torn punk jackets, they were hicks like us.

Daphne and I would have sex anywhere, anytime. She wanted to do it in a cemetery once, so we drove to one and did it in the back of her station wagon.

She had a problem with acne, as did I, and sometimes when we made out, our mouths would inadvertently slurp up all the Neutrogena acne wash and cover-up cream. I thought that her skin problems were probably due to stress. I'm sure it was a burden to always be so horny and to have a dad who was a minister.

One of the last times we had sex was in the middle of my high school football field. We brought a sleeping bag out to the fifty-yard line and squeezed inside. We called it the Human Burrito.

Making the Band

David was one of the other Hermiston kids. He was a stocky grocery store worker, always trying to talk me into starting a New Wave band with him.

Almost every weekend, David and Daphne and whoever else was around would sleep on Marco Torrez's floor. Marco was this guy all my other friends made fun of. He was a tall, black-clad Mexican who wore lipstick and women's hats.

One night, David and Daphne met me at Shari's, one of those twenty-four-hour restaurants that we often found ourselves in since we were too young to go to bars. David kept going on about how he was learning guitar and buying a drum machine. "We could be like the Jesus and Mary Chain," he said. "There're only two guys in that band." David seemed to think I was going to be the singer in his band. "We have to think of a good name and we have to take press photos," he said as he sipped from the oversize milkshake in front of him. I looked at Daphne to try and gauge her position on the matter.

"You should take naked photos," she said. "That would get some attention and create controversy. I could use my uncle's camera. He lives up here."

"That's awesome," said David.

I wasn't sure what to say. I wasn't thrilled by the idea of posing nude for photos but I liked taking my clothes off in front of Daphne.

The following Friday, we met at Marco's before the dance. I'd been to his place only once before. It was a small one-bedroom apartment with big posters of the Cure and Bauhaus looming over the front room. There were black curtains and black candles and a black fake leather couch. David sat in a director's chair, writing band name ideas in a notebook. He told me Daphne was on her way and that her uncle was coming over to help her set up the camera. "Don't worry," he said. "Her uncle is cool. I met him once. I think he used to be a model."

There was a little kitchen in the apartment and I went in there to say hi to Marco. I was hoping nobody else would be there to watch this. Marco was wearing a satin bathrobe and I asked him if he was going out later. He shrugged and took a pizza out of the oven. "I guess we'll see what everyone feels like doing," he said.

"What do you mean?" I said.

"We're all going to do it," he said. "It's going to be cool."

One of Marco's Goth friends came out of the bathroom, a girl named Alexis. I didn't know her very well. She was sort of new in town and over twenty-one. She bought all the alcohol. She was tall and skinny and wore clothes that barely stayed on. She made up her face to look like a china doll. In fact, her whole body looked like it was powdered white. She could glow in the dark. She was probably the first person I knew who wore such sexy clothes. Garter belts. Lace. She probably had to go to Seattle to buy such things. I said hi to her and wondered if she was going to get naked.

Daphne came in with her uncle then, carrying a tripod and an awkward camera. Her uncle was a chubby forty-year-old with a fringed jacket and feathered hair. "Hi everyone," he said, a little too jovially. "This is going to be fun." He helped Daphne set up the tripod in front of the couch. "So, should we do the band photos first or just start with everyone?" asked the uncle. No one said anything.

Daphne turned and snapped a photo of my blank expression. "We have lots of film," she said. "Let's just do some candid shots first. See what develops. Get it? See what develops?" She turned and took a photo of her uncle.

"Oh, God," he said. "Whatever you do, don't let your dad see me in these photos. He'd damn me to hell—again!" Everyone laughed a little about that. We all started drinking then. I put more vodka in my Big Gulp cup, mixing it with the last of my Coke. I liked the burn in my throat. The sensation of almost throwing up with each swallow. Five or six swallows later, I was over that hump. I became loose and daring.

"Shirts off," yelled Marco. He had Depeche Mode on and I was watching Alexis dancing out of the corner of my eye. Five shirts were thrown into the corner.

We looked at the uncle with his striped polo shirt still on. "I'm only here to document," he said. Then he asked Daphne if there was supposed to be someone else there. "I thought you knew an Asian boy," he said. He seemed a little disappointed when Daphne told him that her Asian friend wasn't coming.

Alexis grabbed my arm and led me to the couch. She had on a black see-through bra and I saw her small nipples sticking out a little. "Let's see how tough you are," she said. She had me lie down with my shoulders on the armrest of the couch. She grabbed a burning candle and dripped wax on my chest. It stung just lightly before drying in clumps. I peeled the pieces off my smooth chest and looked at them closely. She tried to make designs on me. A question mark. The anarchy A. There wasn't quite enough wax melted to do them in one try. She straddled me and leaned over with the candle. One of her bra straps was down and I was hoping that she'd move close enough for me to brush my mouth against her breasts but the candle went out and she leaned back, laughing. I remember some things vividly: her bra slipping down a little more as she laughed, the quiver of her body, the anxious erection in my pants.

Daphne lit some more candles and was starting to take photos. She wore a white bra and her breasts looked heavy in it. I noticed a few acne scars on her back. I wanted to look at them closely but I didn't want everyone else to think I was weird. Marco sat by me on the couch and Alexis grabbed another candle and moved over to him. "Let's see if you can take the pain," she said to him. Marco was more lighthearted about the whole thing. He laughed and squirmed and pretended like it was really hurting. I felt sort of foolish and I got up to grab my drink.

David was standing behind Daphne as she paced around and aimed the camera in odd angles toward the couch. He seemed a little stoned or nervous. I got the feeling that he wanted to see Alexis naked too. He fingered the belt loops on his pants and breathed awkwardly as he drank three cans of beer in quick succession. Daphne's uncle eventually tried to sneak out of the apartment, growing disinterested. "Where you going?" Daphne called out. He said he'd see her in the morning, and left without saying good-bye to anyone else. "Oh well," said Daphne. She set the camera down and unsnapped her bra. Alexis and Marco hooted their approval and she kept going. Her socks and pants were tossed sloppily in the corner. David nudged me and we followed her lead.

"Check this out," Marco shouted over the music. He stood up, dropped his pants, and had his penis sticking out the fly of his boxers. The girls laughed. The mood seemed so much lighter after Daphne's uncle left; it almost floated. I saw Marco's penis and it was the first time I had seen someone else's penis. It looked big around the head but the rest of it seemed splotchy and discolored. Daphne took some photos and Marco covered his face, suddenly shy. "I should get it hard first," he said. Then he paused. "Right? We don't want our dicks to look small."

"Nothing looks worse than a dead dick," David said. All of us burst out laughing.

"I'm not helping out in that department," said Alexis. My anticipation was killed a little when she said that.

Daphne's camera turned our way. "Okay, future rock stars," she said. She stood on a chair and took shots of us from above. I put my arm around David and he felt tense. He pushed me away a little and said he had to go to the bathroom to check himself out in the mirror. "We'll use only the best ones!" Daphne shouted after him. She gave me the camera and told me to take over. I wanted to snap a photo of her but she dashed away, following David into the bathroom, saying something about how she didn't like pictures. I thought I heard David getting sick in the toilet.

On the couch, Alexis laughed as she tried to put her bra on Marco. But it wouldn't fit and ended up looking like a weird sling or bandage. I took photos of that, trying to keep Marco's penis out of the frame. Then I took some really close snapshots of Alexis's lips, legs, and breasts. She was drinking a lot and posing with a bottle of cheap vodka that was almost empty. I started to wonder if she might throw up, but she reached behind the couch and grabbed a blanket. I put the camera down and joined them on the couch. I squeezed in between them and Alexis slowly closed her eyes as she turned her back to me. I tried to kiss her shoulders but she shrugged me off. I was starting to feel a little dizzy as well. I felt Marco pressing against my backside. I figured if I was going to make a move on Alexis, I wouldn't be able to get rid of him, so I tried to block him from my mind. I felt his hands on my hips, slowly moving to my penis. All three of us were under the blanket. I wondered what was happening with David and Daphne. I heard the shower in the bathroom.

"She won't let you," I heard Marco whisper. It took me a second to figure out what he said and what it meant. The music had stopped playing but I could hear Janet Jackson being played from somewhere else. Marco's head went under the blanket and I shifted a little. I could still feel

Alexis, warm on one side, as I looked at the ceiling. I felt Marco put me in his mouth, but it hurt and I pushed him off. I turned back toward Alexis and he started to work me with his hand. I stared at Alexis's neck and the spill of her hair on the couch as he touched me more. I moved my hand back and found Marco's penis. I closed my eyes and flipped over. I heard Alexis breathing, slurry and asleep, on one side of me, and I heard Marco, breathing through his nose quickly, on the other side. We both came on the other's hand. We didn't say anything to each other. I heard the shower turn off in the bathroom. I felt frozen and unsure of what to do next. Marco used the blanket to wipe himself off and nodded for me to do the same. I heard Daphne and David exit the bathroom and slip into Marco's bedroom. David looked pale and weak from vomiting. I pretended to fall asleep, hoping Alexis would wake up or flip over to face me. I thought maybe she wasn't really asleep. I thought about the photos I took of her and then I realized that someone else would see them—the person developing the film. I felt a nervous sickness then.

I slipped off the couch and put my clothes back on. I noticed that it was past 2 a.m. by that time. I stepped outside and breathed in deeply. I thought about getting the film out of the camera and taking it. I tried to go back inside, but I was locked out. I pressed my ear to the door but couldn't hear anything. In a way, it sounded like nothing had happened.

Elvia

During the time I was seeing Daphne and hanging out with the other New Wave kids from Hermiston, I met Elvia, a beautiful and quiet Hispanic girl who dressed more conservatively than the rest. I started to talk to her more and more when she made it up to the Tri-Cities on the weekends. Pretty soon, we decided we would be boyfriend and girlfriend. But first, I had to tell Daphne and stop having sex with her. This was tricky because they worked at the same place, a burger joint called Arctic Circle. After news broke about Elvia and I, Daphne was stone cold to us both. I would come pick up Elvia when she got off her shift sometimes and Daphne stared hatefully at us. Soon enough, Daphne's anger boiled over and she spray-painted a message for me on a water tower near the highway exit. It said, KEVIN SAMSEL IS A DICK.

Elvia and I went out for about a year, and even though I had a couple of prior girlfriends, I felt like this was the first girlfriend I could really get into. She was so pretty, with perfect olive-brown skin and thin-but-plump lips that my mouth will never forget. Her face often displayed a sexy pout or a smile so giddy and mischievous that it ignited her whole being. Our sex felt alive and loving and totally open. Plus, she had a mysterious personality that intrigued me.

She lived with white foster parents who were very religious and wouldn't even let her listen to Top 40 music in the house. Once, they threw out all the cassettes that she had hidden in her closet. Even her David Hart cassette. She had cried about that and I tried to ease her pain by making her mix tapes, which were eventually found and thrown out as well.

Her own parents were somewhere not far away, but it was always kind of vague as to why she didn't live with them. Maybe they were too poor.

Sometimes, during the week, because we couldn't see each other, we would write letters. In these letters, she was more goofy than she was in person. She'd crack jokes, make fun of her foster parents, and quote fake Bible passages. If she hadn't lived with such conservative white people, she may have been a Goth or a punk.

One week she sent me a serious letter and told me that she was pregnant. I tried to make a plan to see her that weekend (we'd sometimes sneak long-distance phone calls to each other), but she told me she was grounded. She asked me to send her $300 so she could get an abortion. I emptied out my bank account and scrounged up some more tip money and sent cash. A week later she called me and said she hadn't gotten the money yet. I really need it, she said. She was crying. I told her I'd send it again, but this time it would be a money order. But first I went down to the post office and asked them if the letter had not been sent for some reason. I kicked myself for sending cash and my suspicious mind kept thinking that a crooked mailman probably stole the valuable letter. I could picture him sitting in his mail truck, holding it up to the light and glimpsing the hundred-dollar bills through the envelope.

The people at the post office couldn't solve the mystery for me.

Two days later, with a rock of heavy embarrassment in my gut, I had to call Elvia and tell her that I could send her only $150. She seemed disappointed and cold and then told me that she was probably going to move after her upcoming high school graduation. What do you mean? I asked her. I'll tell you later, she said.

Daphne and the other Hermiston Wavers were still coming up to the Tri-Cities on weekends, but Elvia wasn't catching rides with them anymore. I heard from one of them that Elvia had moved away. I had this person snoop around and a couple of months later, I had a new phone number for Elvia. One in Yakima. Someone thought that she had moved there with a cousin. An older Mexican guy.

I called the number one night when Mom and Dad were gone. I was able to sneak long distance calls on our phone sometimes, even though Dad would get mad about it. Elvia answered. I said hello and her voice answered back, sounding shocked and sad, as if she had been caught stealing something. At first, she seemed regretful that she hadn't spoken to me. I asked her why and she became vague and nervous. I told her that I loved her and that I wanted to come see her. Finally, she told me that she had moved to Yakima to live with a new boyfriend. An older guy I knew nothing about. I asked her all the selfish questions: Why did she do this to me? Were they having sex?

Was the sex better? Did she ever love me? We both started to cry, but I was trying to stay calm.

Mom and Dad drove up the gravel driveway at that moment. I was using the phone in the kitchen, where they were about to enter, arms full of Kentucky Fried Chicken buckets. "Get off the phone. It's time to eat," said Dad. They sat down just ten feet away at the dining room table. I tried to stretch the phone cord into the hallway, but Dad got angry and told me not to pull it so hard. It was already crackly. "It's time to eat!" Dad shouted. It was as if he and Mom had gotten into a fight on the way home. He was in a foul mood.

"Are you going to go to school somewhere there?" I asked.

"I don't think so," she said.

"What are you going to do?"

"I'm going to have babies," she said.

I thought she was saying this to hurt me, to make me give up. "You're going to have babies *with him*?" I said.

Then Dad walked over and pushed his finger on the hang-up button. "Did you hear me?" he said.

"I'm not hungry right now," I said.

I went to my room and paced around, hoping the tension in the house would decrease. I went out to the kitchen again and told them I wasn't feeling well, hoping that would calm things down. Dad bit into a piece of chicken and tore off a chunk of meat. He was the kind of eater who devoured everything to the bone.

As they ate their dinner, I snuck down the hall and into their bedroom, where the other phone was. I picked it up and called Elvia again. She answered after several rings and started crying. I felt like I was now in the position of comforter and I started telling her that things would be okay and that I loved her. I wanted to ask her what she meant when she said the baby thing, but she was too upset to go back to that.

After a few minutes, a man's voice came on. Her new boyfriend. "Just leave her alone," he said. "She doesn't want to talk to you any more."

"Yes, she does," I said. I felt stupid, like I was challenging him to a fight from seventy miles away. "Who are you?" I asked.

"Look, man, it's over. You're upsetting her." He said this like he was trying to be cool. "*C'mon*, dude."

In my head, I tried to imagine her, in this shitty little farm town, crying in the corner of some tiny one-bedroom house. I knew I'd probably never see her again.

I told myself that it wasn't my fault.

Yvette

When I was nineteen, I briefly went out with a black girl from Pasco named Yvette. The first time I saw her, she was wearing a very sexy turquoise dress at a Pasco High School dance. When I introduced her to my brother Matt, I could tell he liked her too and I felt guilty about that.

I went to eat dinner at Yvette's house and the food was totally different from what my family ever had. It was soul food. Her mom even called it that.

She was a virgin and we often talked about having sex and where we should do it.

My cousin Tana gave me a key to her apartment and I often stayed at her place when she was gone. Her fish needed to be fed.

Yvette and I eventually tried to have sex in Tana's bed. It almost seemed too planned out and it was hard to get excited. Yvette said she wanted to do it, but we couldn't make it work for some reason. I was nervous and started to have performance anxiety. Her vagina was slick but felt like a wall. Her hymen would not budge.

I didn't see her for about a month after that. I knew it wasn't working out without her having to tell me. But I saw her one last time at a party in East Pasco. It was at some DJ's house—the kind with weeds and dirt in the front yard instead of grass. Some raw homemade-sounding hip-hop was blaring out of the living room stereo when I came in. Everyone looked at me suspiciously since I was the only white person there. Yvette led me to a dark bedroom and we went in. I couldn't see a thing but I could hear her breathing hard. She reached into my pants and started jerking me off. My pants fell and I could sense her moving down my body as I stood there, surprised and unsure of what to do. I touched her head softly and felt her short blunt hair until I came.

Basement

Right before I moved out of my parents' house to live with friends in Richland, I relegated my suitcase of porn to the basement, a narrow dirt-walled space that had been there since before the fire. I tried to bury it under some saggy boxes and moldy clothes, but my dad found it later. I claimed not to know anything about it. I said it probably belonged to Mark.

The Stilts

My first apartment was at the Stilts, the cheapest housing in the Tri-Cities, in uptown Richland. I lived there for two short months. The first month I was living with three other guys who had decided to move out right as I was moving in. I was the only one there for the second month. The one thing I remember about the Stilts was that it used to be an army barracks or something. There were six rooms in each apartment, with a small kitchen and bathroom. A lot of kids just out of high school lived there and there were always parties.

It was a period of time for me where I tried to exact revenge on the ghost of Pam. I still resented the fact that she was my first real girlfriend. Initially blinded by my pubescent desperation, I eventually realized she was simply a dullard. I regretted all the time I had invested in her, only to have her cheat on me. She instilled in me a precedent that I would constantly rehash—seducing people and then cheating on them. I was guilty of using bodies as I recorded sound bites in my brain—little quotes about how much of a nice guy I was, how cute I was—that I played back in my head to somehow validate my actions and make myself feel good. I was taking advantage of anyone I thought was as weak as me.

Holly

Holly was sixteen when I started going out with her. I was nineteen and trudging through my one and only year of community college in Pasco. I met Holly at the Palace and I was attracted by her combination of toughness and innocence. On the surface, you'd see a leather jacket, torn jeans, wrestling shoes, and jet-black hair spiked into a Mohawk. But she also had the sweetest dimpled smile and she would write mushy love letters to me and invite me to do stuff with her and her mom. She was also a big girl.

I feel bad saying this but I'd feel worse if I lied—I initially went out with her because she was very large-breasted and I wanted to feel her up. A month or so into the relationship, we were ready to have sex. Then I learned that she was a virgin. I knew from my own unfortunate experience with Pam that people usually fall in love with the first boyfriend or girlfriend they have sex with. But I was such a horndog that I decided not to care. The first time happened in her bedroom when her mom was gone. I wasn't too far removed from my virginity either, so it didn't last long. After that, we would have to sneak around different places to have sex and sometimes we'd do it in my Volkswagen Rabbit somehow, once in the parking lot of the community college. When I decided to break up with her a month later, I was suddenly the scum of the scene. All of Holly's friends at the Palace sneered at me, called me an asshole, or just put their noses in the air when I walked by. Holly ignored me as well, but she did so with a face full of disappointment and regret.

The next year, Holly went to her prom with Chuck, a guy I was sharing a small trailer with. It felt like a taunt to see their picture—her standing in front of Chuck, his arms around her chubby waist—displayed on the shelf next to our small TV. This was my punishment for screwing over a virgin.

Taternuts

This is how I learned about cunnilingus from a policeman's wife and became a legendary fryer at the same time.

First off, I was a graveyard waiter at a place called the Top Hat. It was an all-night diner in Pasco, just down the street from where the prostitutes walked around. They'd sometimes come in with their johns and I had to serve them coffee and pie.

On my way home from work, I stopped at a doughnut shop called Taternuts. The reason being, of course, because it was there. And because it was open, which many places weren't at five thirty in the morning.

A man wearing an Ocean Pacific shirt and graced with a mustache as thick as Gene Shalit's was strong-arming a blob of dough on a floured surface near the entrance. I checked out his action over the plastic sneeze guard.

"Whatcha up to?" he asked me. I was wearing a tie and probably looked like I had been out all night drinking.

"Uh, I just got off work. I wait tables. The Top Hat. Graveyard." I moistly chewed out the words, amid cake doughnut debris. "These cake ones are awesome," I said.

"They're called spuddies," he enlightened me.

"What the—"

"We don't make doughnuts here. These are made with

potato flour mix. The cake ones are spuddies and the raised ones are taternuts." He folded up the flattened dough three times and then plopped it atop a machine that fed the dough into a cutter-type roller. "This is taternut dough. It has yeast, so it rises in here." He opened a metal door and showed me some hot racks near his feet. "The spuddie dough doesn't have yeast, so it stays cake." He let me think about this. "Want a job?" he asked me.

A few days later, I went from graveyard-shift waiter to early-morning taternut fryer. It was closer to home, there were free taternuts, and the pay was better. The man I worked with was called Big K. He was about thirty and built like a tight end, about six-three, 240 pounds. Big K's sister was a large woman named Debra and she was real bossy sometimes and real funny at other times. Whenever we got busy, which we did a lot it seemed for just a dough-nut—I mean taternut—shop, Debra would say things like: "Shake yourself" and "C'mon Kev, you want me to take over back there? Gotta get crankin'!"

It was easy to get pissed at her but she knew how to make you work harder. She would have made a great basketball coach. Maybe it was the fact that she was getting married to a cop who came in all the time. You know, it's funny; I never really thought about it until now: a cop marrying a woman who runs a doughnut shop. I mean taternut shop.

Most of the people who came into the taternut shop were people who worked a couple of miles down the road at the Hanford Nuclear Reservation. Also there were lots of teachers, sundry retired folks, suits, and assorted early risers. It seemed like a requirement to like sports if you were a regular. And if you were a regular that also meant having the same thing every day. If Debra saw you coming from across the parking lot (even at a snail's pace) she'd shout out, "Sedale, chocolate taternut and a decaf for Joe. Quick." If a customer came in and his usual diet wasn't set up at his everyday spot there must've been something wrong somewhere. We were a well-oiled machine.

Sports were the reason I became known as Sedale. Big K was a pretty goofy jock kind of guy who was always making funny noises and doing silly pranks. I was mostly into music at the time, but I still had a passing interest in sports clinging to me from my days as a statistics-hoarding football freak in junior high. Big K and I went out after work a few times and played some playground basketball. His stiff but powerful inside play reminded me of Robert "the Chief" Parrish of the Celtics, while my quick, slashing drives and hustle earned me the alias Sedale Threatt, who was a backup point guard for the Philadelphia 76ers.

So we'd be working in the midst of some mad rush and our pace is faster than the taternuts can fry in the fryer and just to keep the mood fun for all, K would shout out my nickname in an exaggerated PA announcer voice: "Sedaaaale Threeeeeeatt!" and then I would go "The Chieeeeeeeef!" All the customers seemed used to these outbursts and even our occasional and random animal noises.

Some customers were also special enough to receive trumpeting treatment. Murphy was one. He was a slouched sixty-two-year-old whom we'd greet by announcing: "It's the Armeeeeeenian!" Other regulars were Ray, Coach,

Betsy Baker, Danny Boy, Ozzie, and Miss Missy. Random terms were rotated for folks we weren't familiar with. Tags like Old Man, Big Dog, Chi Chi, and Buster.

Whenever we had the dough rolling through the cutter, Big K and I had to stand on each side and gather up the uncooked taternut shapes. They'd then go into the warm racks where they would rise, then we'd plop 'em on a wire tray and stick 'em in the fryer, where they cooked in the oil. All the extra dough was rolled into a little football and thrown around the shop when it wasn't busy. For a little joke, we'd sometimes plant a small piece of dough on the ground where we knew that someone would step on it. Stepping on one of these things felt like you were stepping on a small squishy turd. K and I would casually watch over our time bombs and make ticking sounds. Whenever Debra or whoever would step on it, we'd laugh and congratulate each other on our treacherous achievement.

At some point during this job, which I held for a year and a half, Debra started to ask me about my sex life. This was right before I started to see Daphne, and then Elvia. I was getting around, as they say, and sometimes girls would come see me at work.

Debra wanted to make sure I knew a few important things—tools for life—such as the mysterious and tribal-sounding ritual known as "eating out a pussy." All the photos of oral sex I'd seen in magazines were of women giving it to men. I had no idea that oral sex was such an equal opportunity activity. The first time a girl asked me to give her oral sex, it was a one-night stand with a sixteen-year-old devil-worshipping runaway. We were making out and I had her shirt off.

I began licking her breasts and she asked: "Will you eat me out?" I thought about it for a second, knowing I didn't even know the first step, and politely answered, "No, thanks."

My mother and I had too much of an age gap to have sexual talks. I think she knew something was up in regards to my sexual blooming, but she never pried. Mostly she stayed in her sewing room and listened to Nat King Cole as I wrestled with my puberty (and penis) in the next room. I'm sure that some of my family thought I was gay. The Scotch-taped photo of Ralph Macchio on my wall could have been cause for alarm.

Big K was possibly my best bet for sex advice from an older, more experienced person.

"Gotta grow yourself one of these first," he pontificated, sticking his mustache out as far as the tip of his nose. I decided to cut my losses and not explore his wisdom further.

After work that day, Debra cornered me in the back room. "You want me to just tell you how to do it and save ya some time?"

I tried to think of something funny to say, but settled for: "Sure, if you want to."

She explained several things: the taste, the labia, the clit, the secret button, the canal. She mapped out certain methods: the vibrator, the fingers, the tongue, lips, teeth, etc. And finally, she soberly gave me a few warnings: yeast infections, periods, pubic hair in the teeth, gagging on excess pubic hair, pubic hair that seems to be either absent or shaved.

I didn't ask her about how the cop did it to her. Actually, oral sex may have been against state law for all I knew. I made a note to be careful in case it was.

The results were: I loved it!

Even despite close calls with yeasty girls and others who looked like they had Jimmie Walker's head sticking out of their groin, the giving of oral pleasure was high on my priorities list on every date. It was indeed one of the most valuable things anyone has ever taught me. Thanks, Debra!

Soon after these lessons, I was preparing to quit my job and move to Spokane, where I would go to broadcasting school. It was time to hang up my apron and retire from the taternut biz. My last day of work was a tearjerker. "You were a legend in the fry zone, Sedale," reflected Big K on my eighteen months of fabulous frying.

I was glazing up a batch and doing my best Dick Vitale, "It's SHOW TIME, baby!"

Big K splashed water on his face and wiped faux tears from under his eyes. "We're gonna retire your apron, man. It'll hang from the rafters."

I looked at my early-morning work companion with respect.

Murphy rattled through the door. "It's the Armeeeenian," I announced.

Murphy stopped for a moment and asked over the sneeze guard, "This is your last day, isn't it?"

"Yeah, off to the medium city, old man."

"Well, you make one heck of a taternut, kid," he said. Then he paused to let me prepare for some wisdom. "Just remember," he started, "when you get there and get settled, you can't come home again."

Interruption

Before I moved to Spokane, Pam came over to my parents' house to see me one last time. She said she saw my car in the driveway and wanted to say hi before I moved. We went to my old bedroom and I tried to figure out what it was she wanted. She said she heard that her little brother had beaten me up at the mall and that she was sorry.

I got angry and defensive and told her that he didn't beat me up. In fact, I forgot it even happened that summer. He saw me at Columbia Center and stopped me outside the Bon Marché. A few of his friends were with him and he was obviously putting on a show for them, acting cool and tough. He said something about "fucking over" his sister and then threw a wild punch at my neck, which I barely felt. There was an angry surge of heat in my head, but I chose to walk away. He and his friends stood there laughing.

Pam sat on my bed and started to cry. I said it was no big deal. "Don't you want to kiss me?" she said, and then she started kissing me. I kissed her back but didn't say anything. It had been almost two years since that night she sat in someone else's car and saw me waiting for her on her porch.

It was dark in my room and even though my parents were home, I locked my door and let Pam get under the covers with me and we took our shorts off. She was on top of me like a wrestler. She had me pinned. She put me inside her and I felt a sad regret. The last thing I ever wanted to do was accept any form of apology that she offered. She would probably feel like we were even now.

The bed was thumping, but I was trying to be quiet. The one thing that would make me feel worse about this whole scenario would be for Mom and Dad to think Pam and I had made up. My doorknob jiggled and then Dad said from the other side of the door, "Does Pam want to stay for dinner?"

"Hold on a minute," I said.

Then the door opened and Dad stuck his head in, his eyes adjusting to the dark. "You shouldn't lock your door," he said. He lingered a moment as Pam and I lay there frozen. I waited for the door to close, but it didn't. I waited to hear the sound of his feet move back down the hall, but they didn't.

Broadcast School

The first time I lived in Spokane (1988) was pretty brief. I found a cheap apartment next to an old office store that specialized in staplers. It was exciting to live by myself for the first time, but the place got depressing quick. The tiny kitchen had a warped floor and there was a permanent smell of old hamburger. There was a small dirt lot behind the apartment where people from the other seven apartments parked their cars. No matter where I parked, one guy from down the hall would always leave me aggressive notes of complaint.

The radio class that I signed up for at the Ron Bailey School of Broadcasting was only a nine-month course, but it cost about $8,000. I thought it was only a matter of time before I'd be starting a long and interesting career in radio. I dreamed of the day when I could play whatever songs I wanted and everyone would understand how great my taste in music was, like my days as a kid cranking 45s out my bedroom window.

It was the first time I really tried hard in a school setting. I had perfect attendance and my efforts soared above those of the dozen other students. The instructor was a fifty-something guy with the kind of body language that suggested thousands of hours of overnight DJ shifts and a few divorces in his past. No matter how many cups of coffee he slurped, he still seemed in need of a nap. He wore jeans and denim shirts, like the Marlboro Man. I'm guessing that his bushy mustache hid many frowning wrinkles. But he was kind to me and had a smoky smooth voice. After just a couple of weeks, he pulled me aside and asked me if I wanted to start working weekends at the local AM country station.

I was the first one in class to get a job, though it was mostly pushing buttons and reading the weather and call letters once an hour. During the week, I worked as a parking lot attendant.

My old high school friend Maurice called me one day and asked if he could come up and stay with me for a couple of weeks. Ever since graduation, things had been weird with Maurice and me. After being so antidrug, antidrinking during our high school years, Maurice had somehow become a total souse, drinking cheap beer all the time and always passing out or getting sick. I felt like I had to let him stay with me. Maybe it would help to mend our relationship.

Maurice mostly stayed on my couch those two weeks, drinking Stroh's, his cheap brew of choice. He would stack the empty cans on the windowsill and never clean up. I drank with him a few times but he always drank faster. As he got more drunk, he got more mean. Even though he had little experience with girls, he would say the worst things about my old girlfriends, especially Holly, who he called a fat cow.

One night, INXS was playing at the Coliseum. It was

the height of their popularity and Darren came up from the Tri-Cities to go with me to the show. I had an extra ticket for Maurice, hoping that a nice gesture would make his stay more tolerable. I almost begged him to go with us, even just to get him out of my apartment. "No," he said. "I just bought some beer. I'm going to enjoy myself just fine." He stretched out the last two words sarcastically.

Darren and I walked down to the show, barely speaking a word. I looked at the extra ticket in my hand and couldn't believe that Maurice had elected to stay home and drink by himself. There was a strange sad mood in the night air, like a close relative had just died.

Good-bye Soap

On the very last day of broadcasting school, I wasted no time getting out of Spokane. I decided I was going to move to Seattle, where a few of my Tri-Cities friends had moved. There was a Ron Bailey school there too, so I thought they could help me get a radio job.

I packed up my car with the few things I owned at the time (the furniture stayed—it was a "furnished apartment"). I gave the place a quick clean and left my key on the kitchen counter. It was just after midnight, but before I could leave for good, I decided that I would finally leave my own message for the guy down the hall, the one who always complained that I was parking in his spot. I took a bar of soap and wrote some nasty things all over his car. I did it quickly and nervously. I scrawled something like: COME SEE ME! APARTMENT 4. And then I quietly rolled out of there with my headlights off. When I pulled into the street, I turned on my headlights and eventually began to laugh to myself as I got on the freeway to Seattle. I was having some sweet revenge. Too bad no one else could see it.

Seattle

When I first moved to Seattle, I was living with about five other guys in a mess of an old house. I didn't have my own room so I slept in my friend James's room, in his walk-in closet. I was seeing a girl I knew briefly from Spokane. She had worked at a vintage clothing store where I bought a leather motorcycle jacket on layaway. I must have gone through a phase where I had crushes on anyone who looked like a famous actress—this girl looked like Rae Dawn Chong. Her parents were Jehovah's Witnesses and she wasn't allowed to see me, so we snuck around. One night, when her parents were out of town, I went to visit her. She was living with them until she could afford her own place. I was nervous the whole time I was there and kept waking up through the night. There was religious stuff everywhere and photos of the family. Her large black father and her humorless-looking white mother sneered at me judgmentally. I couldn't deal with the stress and eventually broke up with her.

One night, while I was out on a rare barhopping night with friends, I met a girl named Erin. She was skinny and boyish and we joked around a lot, her whole mouth opening with every bright laugh. She was nineteen but had a fake ID that looked nothing like her. Her laid-back hippie demeanor intrigued me and made me feel like I didn't have to impress her—at least that's how I perceived it, being someone who never knew any real hippies. We danced to Fun Boy Three and then went home together. She played Cat Stevens the next morning and made coffee on a stove. I stayed wrapped in her blankets, on the futon on the floor.

I felt right away that I could openly express myself with her and I cried the first morning we spent together. For a while there, I would cry at anything. Songs. Letters. Movies.

(My crying jags would become an initiation for any girl I dated for the next ten years—we'd get to know each other, sleep with each other, and then I would start using her pillow as a handkerchief.)

Three months later, I moved into an apartment with Erin and her best friend, Mary. I had a scooter at the time and Erin and I would ride around at night when we couldn't sleep. She was a very restless sleeper. She even had a strict rule for us in bed. She didn't want to feel my knees touching her, my feet touching her, or my butt touching her. She said the sensation of those body parts felt cold and foreign, like they were dead fish or something. This rule simply became: NO KNEES, NO BUTT, NO FEET (NKNBNF). But I was not annoyed by this. I was charmed.

I also learned that she became easily jealous. She made me burn a pile of some of my old photos one night. We precariously made a bonfire of my past girlfriends on the ledge of our window. She blew the hot ashes into the air as the images melted away.

Clinic

After a year in Seattle, Erin and I moved back to Spokane so she could finish some credits at Whitworth College. I wasn't excited about going back to eastern Washington but I knew I had to go somewhere I could get a radio job. The only DJ job I had in Seattle was with a mobile music company. I'd get hired every other weekend to play records at high school dances, receptions, birthday parties, and old folks homes. Besides that, I worked at a 7-Eleven and then waited tables at an oyster bar in Pike Place Market.

A career in broadcasting meant you had to work your way up from smaller towns to bigger cities, so even though I didn't like Spokane the first time around, I tried to see it as a stepping stone in my radio career. My brother Matt had finished college by this time and he was about to move to Columbus, Ohio, for a sportscaster job after being the sports anchorman in Kennewick for a couple of years. Later, he'd get jobs in Seattle and then Houston—that's how a broadcasting career was supposed to go: small market, medium market, and then big markets. I was hired again at the AM country music station and began filling in sometimes on the FM Top 40 side of the building too. I worked at a record store most of the time though.

Just a couple of months after moving to Spokane, Erin

found out that she was pregnant. Although our relationship was serious, we decided we were too young to have a baby. We solemnly arranged an abortion at a clinic on the other side of town. I drove her there but she didn't want me to go inside. We sat in the car and, without saying a word, we both stared at the building and cried. One of her girlfriends was going to come back and pick her up and take care of her. She needed to be with another woman for that part, she said.

I sat in my car for a while after she went inside. I imagined the uncomfortable waiting room. I imagined everyone trying slyly to catch a glimpse of the other women there. I wondered if that helped each woman, to see the others and for a moment think that at least they weren't alone. I wondered if there were any men sitting in there.

Later, Erin told me how it went. The nurse took her in and weighed her and measured her. They said she was two inches shorter than she is. Erin was unusually bothered about this and argued with the nurse about the two inches until the doctor came in. They got her into position and gave her something to knock her out. "And then I was having a really peaceful dream," she said. "I was walking through a forest and I found a pool of water. I put my hands in the water and was making little waves, like a kid playing. I cupped my hands and lifted some out and watched it drip through my fingers."

Broken

Something happened after that day. I had a sense that all the fun was gone. I was falling out of love and I didn't know why. There was nobody else I was interested in. It was one of the few times I'd ever been monogamous, but I was losing interest.

One night, we were talking about something trivial—a TV show or a band or something—and the conversation suddenly changed. I told her that I thought we should break up. Erin looked at me in disbelief and realized I was serious. "I just don't think we should be together anymore," I said. I didn't have a way to communicate my reasons. We didn't speak much for the rest of the night. She asked me questions and all I could say was "I don't know." Neither of us left that night and we slept one last time in our bed. When we woke up, we had sex, knowing it was the last time.

I went to work and left her at home to make plans for herself. She called me before I got off work and told me that she had taken most of her stuff and had driven to Seattle. She was dropping out of school and staying with her dad. I went home and found a bunch of my clothes and things thrown around. I had a large collection of records and cassettes and it looked like she had thrown a bunch of them against the wall. I spent all night cleaning up.

I couldn't figure out what I was doing after that. I missed Erin, but she was not coming back. I felt like a zombie but I had to put myself back together enough to find a new, cheaper place to live. I couldn't stay in that apartment much longer. Andrew, a friend from the Tri-Cities who lived in Seattle, called me and told me that Erin and a couple of her friends had stayed in his apartment on New Year's Eve. He said that Erin was with an old boyfriend and that he could hear them having sex while he was trying to sleep. I went out that night and found a sex shop with those little movie booths in the back. This was the start of a habit that lasted a few years.

This part of the store was dark, with only some small red lights over each station that was being used. One man lingered in the corner, like he was waiting for someone. I walked over to one of the empty booths and paused for a second and looked at him before going in. I left the door unlocked and took out some dollar bills. I heard the man try the doorknob and then the door opened and he snuck inside with me. The rules posted in the store started with "1. Only one person per booth."

"Can I watch?" he asked. He didn't say what he wanted to watch, but I knew.

I was nervous and I couldn't get the machine to take the first dollar. It kept sliding back and forth like a tongue sticking out at me. I could hear the man breathing behind me. Finally, the dollars slid into the machine and the TV screen came to life. I pushed the button to change the channel until I found one I liked. I had my pants undone and so did the man.

"Can I touch you?" the man asked.

"Yes," I said.

He was standing beside me now and I looked back and forth between the man's hand on my dick and the screen. I reached over and held his cock in my hand and starting moving it. I felt something strange so I looked closer at him. He was skinny and slightly hunched. His face was thin, with high, almost feminine cheekbones. There was no hair anywhere on his cock and he wore a leather thing around it. A cock ring, I guessed.

We didn't say another word until we were done. He left me there and slipped back into the dark hallway. My time was not up yet. I stood there, surrounded by cum on the floor, watching the TV, flickering with moans and skin, until it shut off.

Acid

I stayed in Spokane after the breakup and met a new friend named Vincent Price, with whom I had my first acid experience. That night was so much more memorable—and positive!—than the first time I had sex. Part of the downtown area was sectioned off, and makeshift basketball courts were everywhere. We found a ball and played in the dark for a few hours, laughing hysterically. Then, out of nowhere, some kids—they seemed to be about thirteen years old—drove up to us in two golf carts. They offered us rides, and we got in and let them speed us through Riverfront Park on the walking trails. The headlights weren't too strong, and we almost crashed a few times before they dropped us off by our bikes.

We rode to a Safeway around five in the morning and bought orange juice, because Vince said it was "good for visuals." We sat on the curb outside and watched the painted handicap symbol on the pavement bubble and expand. It was glorious.

Around eight in the morning we were finally ready to sleep a little. We rode our bikes over the little bridges of downtown Spokane. Our bodies seemed to be humming a song no one else could hear.

The Outlaw

I **worked at** the radio station on weekends and, after quitting the job at the record store, at a Tex-Mex restaurant called The Outlaw during the week. There were only five others who worked there and four of them were family. A husband, wife, brother, and son. The son was only about thirteen but he hung out there a lot, sometimes doing homework and helping out with the dishes when it got busy. The brother, who was the main cook, would sometimes have diabetic seizures and the rest of us would have to make him drink orange juice. The drinks were served in glasses shaped like old cowboy boots.

I remember being really impressed about how the husband ran the family business with such an easygoing nature. He was always telling his wife that he loved her and called his son honey or sweetie. It was the first time I heard a dad call his son names like that and it caught me off guard, especially because I thought the son would protest or be embarrassed. But he wasn't. They were a close family. Whenever I saw a family like that anywhere, I would watch them carefully, as if they were a rare species of animal. I would want to go and join them. Feel that unbreakable bond.

I remember thinking that if I had a son, I would call him honey.

Dog Grave

When I first moved away from the Tri-Cities, Mom and Dad kept my dog, Scooter, for a while and then decided to give him away. He was about eight years old. Dad placed an ad in the paper and one couple responded to take him. Scooter went to live with this couple somewhere out in the country.

A couple years later, Dad decided to covertly check on him. He found out where the family lived and drove out there. He saw Scooter, chained up in a big empty backyard, and felt bad for him. Scooter saw him and ran toward him but couldn't reach Dad's hand. He wagged his tail and whimpered and barked. Dad told him that he'd be back to see him again soon.

The next week, he went back out and saw Scooter again. This time, the man who had taken him was there, working in the front yard. Dad talked to him and realized that the man and his wife had not given Scooter the attention and freedom that they promised. He talked the man into giving Scooter back.

Mom called me the next day and told me Scooter was back at home with them. She told me the story about Dad getting him back and I tried to imagine the whole thing. I went to Kennewick for a visit soon after that and played with Scooter a lot. I was sad and confused as to why they got rid of him in the first place, so this reunion felt like a second chance that I never thought I'd get. I realized that this was something rare and that I was lucky. I thought about all the people who loved their dogs until they died and how they probably all had dreams about playing with their dogs one last time. Sometimes you don't know when that last time will be.

Scooter seemed the same to me, maybe just a little slower and older. Some gray hairs around his nose and mouth. I talked to him in a funny dog voice—part Scooby-Doo, part baby talk. I told him that I loved him and that he was always my best friend.

About a year later, Mom told me that Scooter was sick and they took him to the vet, who found cancer in his stomach and said he would have to be put to sleep. I was too far away and too broke to come back to Kennewick. Two days later, they went to the vet for the final time.

Dad took Scooter's body, wrapped in his favorite dog blanket—one that I had given him when he was a puppy—and drove to some hills somewhere between Kennewick and Walla Walla. It was close to a highway that he had worked on and a place he once took Scooter to run free. He dug a grave, buried him, and said a prayer.

Big Dipper

It almost seemed easy for a while. Vince and I would walk around as the third band played and nonchalantly steal as much beer off tables as we could. By that time of night most people at the Big Dipper were juiced up beyond awareness anyhow. It was economical and mischievous. Sometimes the people would be standing just inches away as we emptied their bottles or pitchers into our glasses. During the encore we'd find some girls to scam on and were pretty lucky most of the time, even if it just meant making out for five minutes in a Denny's parking lot. There was one girl named Alison who always went out with band guys. One night she was standing at the bar looking bored while some punk band played for ten people out on the floor. Vince was daring me to go kiss her and she looked over at us and kind of smiled. "She knows what we're talking about," Vince said. Alison looked over at us and kind of laughed, even though she couldn't hear us. Vince had slept with probably more girls in Spokane than I had. Finally I slid out from behind our table, banging my knees and sloshing our pints, and stumbled over to Alison. I didn't really know her at all; she was just a girl I'd see at the clubs all the time, and to her I was just some guy who drove his motorcycle in the snow. "I'm bored," she said. I leaned down toward her and reflexively she turned her mouth up to me and we shared an unbridled fifteen-second kiss.

Empty Nest

At some point in the late eighties, after I left home, Mom and Dad went to visit Elinda, who was living in a community housing project in Seattle. Elinda had arranged for Mom to go with her the next day to the Museum of Flight. Dad was irate at not being invited, and after everyone went to bed, Elinda heard the loud bang of a fist hitting something in the next room.

Gentle Dental

I **wasn't blaming** anyone but myself. I had bad teeth.

I could blame the numerous candy bars stolen from the grocery store across the street from my parents' house. I could blame my parents for being burned out, raising five children before me, and not paying attention to a damned thing I ever did, much less make me brush my teeth. I could blame the mean orthodontist who scolded me too lightly for not brushing, not wearing my rubber bands, not changing my rubber bands often enough, letting them snap in my mouth from time to time. No, it was simply my fault, and I regretted my actions.

Having a root canal could be enough to convert you to a new religion. I'd always thought that death by dentistry would be the most awful way to go—worse than being burned alive or drowning—some guy grinding a syringe into your jaw while you slobber all over yourself with that burned clay taste on your tongue.

When I saw the Yellow Pages ad for Gentle Dental, I was immediately swayed. My job gave me insurance and as much as I wanted to avoid it I knew it had to be done. I was popping about eight aspirin a day to combat my toothache, and had all but stripped any chewing duties from the left side of my mouth.

Once in the chair, I was given the option of wearing headphones. It was when dentists were doing these "extra" things for patients, and because I didn't want to have to make small talk with the dentist and his assorted assistants while they stuck their fingers and metal tools in my mouth, I said yes. One of the assistants, who looked like Joyce De-Witt from *Three's Company* and seemed to purposely rest her chest on my right arm as she scraped my teeth, eagerly told me about a new "virtual reality" system they had just installed. Being pro-anything that would distract me from whatever pain I was about to endure, I said sure. I didn't know what I was getting into, but I pictured skiing down steep slopes covered in soft snow or maybe parachuting out of an airplane. Instead, what I had to choose from were *A Motown Tribute to Smokey Robinson*, a Final Four basketball game from three years before, and a walking tour of Italy. The assistant fished out some embarrassing goggles and plugged them into a machine that looked like a VCR. I put on the headphones and goggles and wondered how the hell they were going to maneuver around them. I saw the stage at the Apollo in the goggles but it wasn't even 3-D and the picture seemed annoyingly fuzzy. I could hear the opening beats of "Going to a Go-Go" but it wasn't in my headphones. It was coming from elsewhere in the room and I wasn't sure what was going on. The dentist and his assistant started working on my mouth and, under the impression that I was being thoroughly entertained, pretty much ignored me. I wondered if they had numbed me yet and started to grow panicked. They stretched a piece of rubber around my ailing tooth and framed it with a couple of cold metal bars that rested uncomfortably on my face. I couldn't tell if it was Smokey Robinson on the stage or not, the reception of the goggles was crap. The dentist sang slowly and menacingly along, thinking that I could not hear him. I grunted a few times and the assistant asked me if the goggles were working, if everything was okay. I couldn't say anything so I made a nuh-uh sound with my throat. She pressed her breasts into me and lifted the headphones from my ears. "Maybe these aren't plugged in," she said. I heard the dentist get up and leave and then her tinkering around with certain wires on the virtual reality machine. Finally, there was music coming from the headphones and she put them back on my ears. I squinted to see what was going on in the goggles and saw a close-up of Elton John, complete with feathery sunglasses. The music in the headphones was nice and clear but I instantly realized it was not going with the visuals. I heard mandolins, fiddles, some piano. Elton John was really getting into it, whatever it was, but I heard someone speaking Italian instead. It must've been the walking tour of Italy.

The dentist returned and patted me on the shoulder. I could see him under the bottom of the goggles. I grunted a little. "You want me to turn up your headphones?" the assistant asked. I lifted my hand slightly and pointed down. "Turn it down?" I nodded as much as I could and the volume went low enough that I could hear the Motown show playing on a small speaker somewhere else. The dentist was singing along again. This time with the Four Tops. I tried to drift off. I closed my eyes and concentrated on Joyce DeWitt. I had always liked Joyce DeWitt more than the others. The rubber thing stretching across my mouth and cheeks was wet with my numb gum slobber. I was almost queasy. George Michael was singing a blue-eyed soul version of "Tears of a Clown." I opened my eyes a little and noticed that he was wearing sunglasses too. "That George Michael can sure sing, can't he?" the dentist commented to himself. "Hhmmph," said the assistant.

Spokane Girls

At my worst, I was seeing three different girls, with my eyes on a fourth.

First there was a sad and mysterious redhead named Ingrid, who gave me a ride home once and later began sneaking me into her basement bedroom, with her parents sleeping above us. The only social thing we did was go to her friend Molly's apartment to drink beer. There would be the three of us plus Molly's boyfriend and some army guy who was always trying to scam on Ingrid. They'd sit around and talk about their favorite local bands and listen to Operation Ivy.

Only a day or two after I started seeing Ingrid, I got together with Lisa, whom I was infatuated with because she looked like Sherilyn Fenn. I walked her home one night and nervously held her hand. I knew she was going out with a really dumb bass player and I tried to convince her that writers made better boyfriends. She said she had a secret dream of being a children's book author. It was a romantic notion, but ultimately sad. She didn't even know who Maurice Sendak was.

The third victim of this triangle was Laura, who was the only real poet I met in Spokane. She worked as a nurse, and

I met her one night at a club where I was preparing to do a poetry reading. She wore stretch pants with skeletons on them and said her favorite bands were T. Rex and the Stone Roses. I wasn't physically attracted to her, but her personality intrigued me more than the others and she had a round face that made me want to cup it and kiss it softly. During my reading that night I played a cassette deck on the stage with the mixed sounds of industrial scrapings and an audience laugh track. I turned this up loud and stripped down to my boxers. I went out the side door of the Big Dipper and walked around the block like that. When I reentered two minutes later, I had a bag of candy and passed it out to the audience. Then, back onstage, I put my clothes back on. During that time, before I even began to read from my erratic pile of rants and poems, Laura said she fell in love with me.

Of course, there's always an outside disruption, something, someone, that will not let you rest easy, will not let your loins settle down and concentrate on just one (or two or three) person(s). But Sarah, a punk girl who walked tall along the downtown sidewalks, with the high black leather boots and short spiky blond hair and perfect European model lips, would not take me seriously.

Sarah was young, independent, smart, and somewhat aloof with the popular boys in the band scene. Everyone knew she was unique and maybe the sexiest girl in town, but she seemed to be holding out for someone special. Not your usual Spokane dude—a Rainier-swigging, pot-smoking tattooed boy—but someone different. And sure,

Spokane had its group of weirdo "other" artist types—guys who turned their warehouse apartments into Goth-rock haunted mazes for Halloween, that tall Asian-looking guy who made short films of people squirming around in bathtubs full of pudding, and even that band who used lawnmower engines to simulate a symphony.

But I was the only young guy in town who was publishing his poems and doing readings at rock clubs. I was unique and maybe a little bit insane. Someone once called me the Poet Laureate of Spokane.

Still, Sarah was cool as crushed ice, and even though we became friends and confessed guilty pleasures to each other (she liked Seal, I liked Suzanne Vega), her demeanor was never flirty and she became the subject of much unrequited lust poetry.

I thought I could be happy with Lisa. I thought I could be with her and let the others slide to the sides. But being perpetually lonely, bored, and horny was a burden.

When Lisa wanted a night out with her gossipy friends, I would find myself running into Laura at one of the two good clubs and going home with her. She lived only a block from me, so it was also convenient. We could practically yell each other's names out our windows.

Or Ingrid would call me, wanting a ride to Molly's apartment. One night, while sitting around at Molly's, I caught Ingrid and the army guy kissing in one of the rooms. I know I had no right to be mad but it caught me off guard and I left. A few nights later, at a party somewhere on the outskirts of Spokane, in some barn somewhere, one of Ingrid's friends started yelling at me about how I was such a jerk and how I made her get together with the army guy. It was so dramatic. I thought I was going to get my ass kicked.

The nights I spent in Lisa's little apartment were great and made me feel like I was in a real relationship. We would sleep in together and she would make espresso in this tiny machine in her kitchen. In fact, she was always making espresso, even at night. We'd lie in bed, listening to Galaxie 500, and sip our homemade lattes. When we'd have sex, I could taste espresso all over her body. It seemed to ooze from her skin. Before I moved out of Spokane though, in the summer of 1991, Lisa went incommunicado on me. She thought she was pregnant and wasn't sure how to talk to me about it. But she wasn't pregnant, and a few years later I would see her again and she was still the same giggly girl from before, which, for some reason, didn't seem quite right.

My connection with Laura was odd. Since she was a poet, I began to feel more for her than any of the others. We actually said to each other: I love you. She had no confidence in herself and her writing, but I published a book of her poems because I thought they were great and disturbing in a quiet, simple way. Later, after leaving Spokane, I would lose touch with her. A few times I've met people who remind me of Laura or maybe look a little bit like her. I am instantly drawn to that person and it makes me feel a little sad or foolish.

A few years ago I got a postcard that was not signed but I'm almost certain it was from her. It said: *I remember walking to and from our beds. The nights turned into mornings. Do you remember LIVING in Spokane?*

Arkansas

I moved to Arkansas when I was twenty-four. I don't really have a sensible reason except I was getting bored of Spokane and wanted to try something totally different. Of course I didn't just poke a blind finger on a map. Paul, a guy I went to broadcasting school with, had gotten in touch with me and said I could get a job at an all-news radio station in Fort Smith, Arkansas. I had never liked Paul and was a little surprised that he even graduated with me, but his offer sounded like a good chance to get more of a full-time radio job.

I packed most of my stuff into my friend Stephen's Dodge Omni and we asked Vince if he wanted to join us on a road trip. Stephen and Vince had been my best friends and confidantes during my stint in Spokane. I had made music, shot films, wrote poetry, and rode motorcycles with them. Just a couple of months before I decided to move, I had a breakdown in Stephen's car and told him that I felt like we were drifting apart. He had been the first person to take me seriously as a writer, even when I wrote garbage. I didn't want to lose him.

The three of us drove to the Oregon coast, down Highway 101 to San Francisco, then to Las Vegas, Arizona, Texas, New Orleans, Memphis, and, finally, Fort Smith,

Arkansas. Stephen wouldn't do acid but Vince and I dosed a few times on the trip.

When we arrived in Fort Smith, Stephen and Vince dropped me off at Paul's house. I hadn't seen him since broadcasting school and he had since gotten married to a girl in our class he'd been going out with. I always thought they were a weird couple. She was a hyperactive New Waver and he was a tobacco-chewing oaf who made fun of the other students even though he could barely speak into a mic without twisting his tongue. When they moved to Arkansas, he dropped out of radio to pursue a window-washing business while she did news at a low-ranking AM station. He'd gotten her pregnant and she had developed this unhealthy infatuation with Reba McEntire. There were posters of her everywhere and cassettes played constantly throughout the day while I tried to read Camus or Dostoyevsky or whatever I was reading back then. Sylvia Plath probably. She also owned a collection of Reba T-shirts.

I soon found out that the radio job I thought had been offered to me wasn't going to happen and I had to find other work. I stayed with my ex-classmates in their trailer home and rationed myself a couple of dollars a day before I became officially broke. Most of that money seemed to be spent at a cheap bakery I found that sold glazed doughnuts for fifteen cents a piece. Eventually I got a job at a factory assembling baby cribs and I was able to move into my own place. That job lasted a month before I became a busboy at a Mexican restaurant called El Chico in Central Mall.

In the meantime, I had bought a used ten-speed and would cruise the small downtown area in search of any kind of youth culture. When I lived in Spokane I went out every other night and I was anxious to find a social life in my new city. I was starting to wonder if moving to Arkansas was a mistake. When I asked people about fun places to go, they'd always say Tulsa or Dallas.

I found out about a place called the 700 Club, a warehouse-type space where local punk and alternative bands played. They had an open mic night coming up and I was eager to go. When I got there that night, it turned out that whoever had the keys to the place hadn't show up. So one of the club regulars put the tailgate of his truck down and made that the stage. It was a humid late-summer night and unlike the Spokane open mics, most of the people who came to the 700 Club (or at least its parking lot) were there with acoustic guitars. It was more like a punk hootenanny.

There wasn't any kind of sign-up list. After someone played a few songs they'd just ask the couple dozen people there who wanted to be next. I watched three or four people strum and sing before I felt like I could get up there. I stood in the bed of the truck and read a few poems. At the time, I was heavily influenced by a Seattle writer named Jesse Bernstein, who wrote violent and funny stories and read them in a crazed scratchy panic. I did my best to imitate Bernstein's voice as I read my own attempts at dark humor. I prefaced my reading by telling everyone that I had just moved there from Washington State. Afterward, a few people talked to me, mostly to ask about the Northwest. Apparently, the video for Nirvana's "Smells Like Teen Spirit" had debuted just the night before and a couple of the kids at the open mic couldn't stop talking about it.

They couldn't believe it when I told them I saw Nirvana play once in a parking garage.

One of the girls there was what I always envisioned a sweet Southern girl would be like. She was warm and pixielike, with dark hair, dark eyes, and a face that glowed with honesty and hope. The only thing missing was the Southern accent. I talked with a few of the guys there and they all acted like they wanted to date her. She had gotten out of a long relationship recently and they were just trying to figure a way to ask her out. After two more open mics, I finally worked up the nerve myself.

We started dating and fell in love. I felt a little weird since she was still in high school, but as soon as she graduated, we decided to move to Portland, Oregon. We ran an espresso cart business and I started publishing more of my writing in magazines. I also met many more writers and began publishing more books by other writers. Even though I was happy, I felt anxious. My girlfriend and I had our ups and downs. There were breakups and infidelities and apologies. There was a miscarriage that I didn't know how to handle. I was unfairly distant and selfish.

But then we got back together and my son was born.

Zach's was a home birth, just after midnight on the hottest day of the year in 1994. The next morning, going out the front door and walking to the store, the world did indeed feel totally different. The sky looked larger and gravity felt nonexistent. I noticed every color and every movement around me. I didn't know much about babies or how to be a father yet, but I knew right away that I was going to do better than my own father.

Aneurysm

Nearly fourteen years after I became a father, I got a message about my own dad. It was from a cousin or aunt, someone I'd never met. She was using that uncertain voice that people use when they're not sure if their message is being recorded. "Kevin? It's about your dad. He had a brain aneurysm and he's in the hospital. They're not sure if he's going to last much longer. Your mom wanted me to call some people and tell them. If you want to see him, or say good-bye, you should probably come right away."

I knew that this was a call I'd be getting soon. For his last four years he was in a wheelchair and everything about him was shutting down. I would call home and talk with Mom about various things and then she'd hand the phone to Dad. It was obvious that speaking had become harder for him. Slowly and with little volume, he would try hard just to get one sentence out, probably about a chore around the house he would never get to or something about church. The words barely made it above the pained breathing. His voice was an eerie death rattle coming through the phone line.

And now this came through the phone line. I played the message over a few times and then saved it.

I was at home in Portland, a four-hour drive away. I

had no desire to go right away. I was about to go to work anyway.

I called Mom and talked to her. She said he was brain dead but still breathing. I asked if he was responding to anything, if he could hear her. The phone line was crackling and cutting out and she couldn't understand what I was saying. I had been waiting for him to die, and had even fantasized about it, but I couldn't help feeling anxious now that it was really happening.

"Can he hear you? Can you talk into his ear?" I asked.

"What's that?"

"Can he understand words?"

"I'm sorry, Kevin. I can't hear what you're saying."

"Could you tell him I love him," I finally said. I was starting to cry.

"Maybe you should take some days off of work," she said gently.

I knew I wasn't going to drive up there until he died. I didn't want to take the days off work and hang out in Kennewick on a deathwatch. The place made me depressed more than nostalgic. Mom and Dad had moved out of the big house we used to live in, the one we rebuilt after the fire. They bought a much smaller manufactured home out behind Columbia Center Mall in the mid-nineties and Mark was still there too, living with them. He was Dad's caregiver the last few years, doing everything from getting him out of bed each day to driving him around. Sometimes Mark and Dad got into arguments and Mark would disappear somewhere for a few days. A few times, Dad himself would try to disappear, cruising in his electric wheelchair along the side of some busy road, going who knows where, until a police officer would stop him and call Mom to come pick him up. I had to laugh the first time I heard about one of these runaway attempts.

I decided to stay in Portland and wait it out, pretend business as usual. I wasn't going anywhere until the heart stopped beating, until the funeral was set.

The Viewing

Dad died a couple of days later and I drove up to Kennewick.

The day before his burial, I went to the funeral home to see Dad in his coffin. I went with Dad's sister Evelyn and her husband, Rolando. I remember meeting Evelyn a couple of times when I was a kid but I had never met Rolando before. They lived around Washington, D.C., most of my childhood and there was some tension on Dad's side of the family because Rolando was black.

Despite the early disapproval of others, they have been married for more than fifty years and have several children and grandchildren. I heard that Dad's family didn't like to advertise that they had a mixed marriage among them. I don't recall Dad ever mentioning Rolando.

One of Evelyn and Rolando's children became an airplane pilot though and that fact became worthy of mention for Dad when he talked with others. "My nephew is a pilot for that airline," he would say, as if he had some hand in this success.

Evelyn is very religious and as we walked into the funeral home she was quietly praying and making the sign of the cross. Rolando, a large man with a kind nature, gently touched her back as they walked. Some piped-in music greeted us in the room that kept Dad's coffin. It was the beginning of viewing hours and I was a little surprised that there was no one else there. Evelyn and Rolando stood back and prayed as I looked closely at my father. His hands looked thin and smudged with spots, as if they had been flattened in some sadistic way. His head was like a skull with fake waxy skin molded around it. I thought I'd see some kind of evidence of the brain aneurysm that finally killed him, but I didn't know what to look for. What little hair he had was swept across his scalp like the faint suggestion of a haircut. His forehead was the only thing that looked strong and real. I looked at him for a few minutes, wondering if I could see myself, but I couldn't. I moved my hand to his head and watched my fingers rest on his forehead. I petted his forehead and thought how strange it was to touch my father this way. I started to cry a little, though I didn't want to. My sniffling gave me away and Evelyn came to my side and touched my arm lightly. She started to talk about how he was in Heaven and that God was taking care of him now, or something like that. I was more annoyed than comforted by her. I looked down at his chest. He was dressed in a dark blue suit with a blue-and-silver tie and the kind of light blue button-up shirt that he would sometimes wear while working in the yard. His chest looked wide but caved in. I stared there, where his heart would be, and watched for any movement. Any sign of a soul.

No Eulogy

The next day, toward the end of my dad's funeral service, the priest asked if anyone wanted to say some words or share a fond memory of my dad. I have not attended many funerals in my life, but I know that this is usually the most emotional and interesting part of the service. Some people think that God lets you watch your own funeral to see what people say before he takes you up to Heaven or gives you to Satan or whatever.

There was an awkward moment when no one approached the podium. Then one of the two older nuns at the service went up and started talking about how helpful my dad was. "Whenever we needed to use a truck, John was always willing to help," she said.

In his last several years, my father was an usher at the church. I think he even did it in his wheelchair for a while. Most of the priests and nuns and churchgoers knew him. A few days before the funeral, someone from the parish told my mom that the church, which holds about 150 people, would probably be full for the funeral. There were about 30 people there.

As the nun talked more about my dad, she shifted from "John was always there for the church" to "John was also a family man who loved his wife and children." Even under the roof of the church where I had spent so many Sunday mornings, my bullshit detector went off. This was a woman, a child of God, who had no idea.

When she was done speaking, there was another uncomfortable pause in the service. I glanced discreetly at Mom and saw that she had no intention of approaching the altar. Elinda sat next to Mom, holding her hand. I thought about going up myself but I couldn't think of anything to say.

One of the only good memories I have of my father are of the times when we'd go to some river or creek somewhere and I would gather agates or any other cool rocks. The year before he died, when I remembered to send him a Father's Day card, I had mentioned these memories. It was one of the few times I wanted to give him something genuine. I knew that he was getting closer and closer to his end.

I stayed seated in my pew, unsure about my ability to speak. I did feel an emotional tug, a burst of tears ready to fall, but they couldn't make it over whatever hurdles were there in my heart. I imagined myself in the casket. My funeral. What people would say. I imagined all of this selfishly, to bring tears, but that didn't work either.

Matt sat next to me, also thinking about what he would say. He told me after the service that he thought about getting up and saying that John was a flawed man, a lonely, disappointed person who wanted forgiveness. He thought about announcing his forgiveness. But maybe the silence was more suitable.

My brother Russell eventually stepped up and started speaking. It seemed like he was up there merely to take up the slack for those of us who had nothing good to share. His words were cautious and faintly praising. He said, "John was a good provider." But, I wondered, of what?

After

After the service, everyone filed out the front doors of the church and we each said hello to the priest and shook his hand. Some people thought there was going to be an open casket and a chance for people to see my dad one last time, but the casket stayed closed. I got the feeling that people felt awkward about it and didn't want to ask if the casket could be opened. There was an anticlimactic feel to the whole thing.

Before the service, Matt, Russell, Mark, and I had to carry the casket from the hearse into the church, and now we had to carry it back out. It was heavier than I thought it would be and the handles felt like they were made of hard plastic. They dug into my fingers uncomfortably. It was as if Dad wanted to give us, the kids, one last moment of discomfort. I could imagine him purposely picking out the heavy one with crappy handles.

With Dad back in the hearse, we gathered on the church steps to figure out who was driving with whom to the cemetery. Then Mom stumbled down the church steps, and even though I was holding her hand, she fell awkwardly on her side. Some relatives I didn't know helped me get her up and she said she was okay, just clumsy.

A short line of cars followed the hearse out to the cemetery. Like a tragically comic movie, it had begun raining and the wind began whipping around like it does in a desert city. At the cemetery, we again had to carry the coffin, this time to the grave. I hadn't brought a jacket and I was pretty cold. I could barely hear the last formulaic words of the priest and I just wanted to get back in my car. I saw the backhoe behind the crowd, behind a tree, like it was an animal trying to hide from us.

Olive Garden

That night, a bunch of the family met at an Olive Garden for dinner. I felt a nagging sense of shame that we went to such a cheerful place. Its peppy waitstaff gave the illusion that the world is a fair and happy place and no one ever dies.

I sat next to my cousin Terry, who is about ten years older than me. I didn't know him that well. He asked me about living in Portland and said he sometimes visited there to go to bookstores. He was a history teacher at a high school in Walla Walla and had a room in his house just for his library. There aren't too many people in my family whom you'd call literary, so I was excited to have someone to talk books with. The conversation soon turned to family though. We played connect the dots with the bloodline. His mom was my dad's sister, Evelyn, who had spent time at Medical Lake, being treated for psychosis at the same time Elinda was there getting shock treatments. His dad was someone he never knew. Apparently, he was a drug dealer who was shot and killed in their front yard when he was a little boy.

He asked me in all earnestness, "How was it growing up with John?" I could tell he knew the answer wasn't going to be good, and I could also tell that he had his own opinions to share.

"It was kind of crappy," I offered.

He nodded and said, "I used to go to your place a lot when you guys were little and I just wondered how you guys dealt with him. He was a bastard."

I ordered another Spanish coffee and we talked more as we ate. By this time, I was tired of everyone treading softly and pretending that Dad's life was saintly. "It's nice to know that there's someone here who isn't full of shit," I said to Terry. I was actually starting to feel like Dad's death would become a reason for the family to open up more. After all, if there's someone in your family whom you're always afraid of offending, it can be stifling for everyone involved. Terry told me about being a kid and going to visit my dad a few times with his mom. This was a couple of years before I was born, when Matt was a baby and Mom and Dad were split up. Dad was living in some kind of motel out by the airport in Kennewick and there were *Playboys* scattered around. One day, after hearing that he didn't get a job that he'd been hoping for, Dad got so angry that he trashed the place, knocking holes in the walls and breaking furniture. He grabbed a gun and went outside and shot bullets into the hard ground.

Matt heard us talking about Dad and joined in the conversation. Soon we were joking and laughing about his spazzy temper and creative cursing. Matt and I tried to remember the exact order of f-words and other swears when he smashed his fingers moving the fridge down the stairs. It's the closest we got to a eulogy.

Hotel

That night, I stayed in a hotel room with my older brother Russell. I was in bed, with the lights out, falling asleep, when Russell said, "I was surprised to hear how negatively you spoke of your dad today." He must have been referring to some of the things he heard at the restaurant.

At first I thought he was going to scold me for that, but I told him frankly about how disappointing a father he was. I talked calmly for fifteen minutes about all the reasons. In a way, Russell reminds me of Dad, so I wasn't sure whose side he would take.

I was surprised to hear him respond with similar stories and feelings. I listened to Russell's voice in the dark and could feel the pain in the air around us. I had always thought of Russell as the serious-minded, conservative, military, older brother, but now I could see that he was vulnerable too. I told him about how having a bad father made me try to be a good father and he told me about some of the things he, too, learned as a father. He had a son named Charles when he was much younger, with a woman he was not with for long. When the relationship ended, he let her take his son. Now, after years of having not talked to him, he had no idea where his son was.

After he lost contact with his son, Russell fell in love

with a Korean woman and married her. She had two children from a previous marriage, a son and a daughter, and Russell became their father. A couple of years into the marriage, his wife was in a car accident and was paralyzed. She's been in a wheelchair ever since. They went back and forth from Korea to America and maintained a strong and loving relationship. But still, I got the feeling that Russell was regretful about not staying in touch with his son.

We talked for a couple of hours and then fell asleep. At five in the morning, the alarm went off and Russell had to get up to catch a flight. I stayed in bed, half-asleep, and said good-bye to him. He set his bags in the hallway and stood in the doorway. "Well, it was really good to talk to you," he said. "And I want you to know that I love you and I'm proud of you."

"Golden Child"

My brother Mark, the "golden child," is the only one in the family that has never lived outside the Tri-Cities. I think about how soul-crushing that must be. The few times he has driven Mom to visit me in Portland, he doesn't want to go anywhere or to explore the city. It's as if nothing interests him. When any of our relatives visit the Tri-Cities, he usually disappears and does not answer his phone. I have noticed that just in the past couple of years, many of his teeth have fallen out and his glasses are usually dirty and broken. His bedroom, across from the bathroom in Mom's home, is always riddled with clothes, electronic things that have been taken apart, Budweiser posters, and weird smells. When he is around, it is surprising if he speaks beyond a few mumbled words.

He was the only one I saw crying at Dad's funeral.

The Day After

The day after the funeral, Mom wanted to have some one-on-one talks with each of her visiting boys—Russell, Matt, and me. Gary did not come to the funeral and wasn't at our family reunion a few years before. He was living in Ohio and working as a truck driver. I haven't seen him in twenty years and it seems like he has been avoiding the rest of the family as well.

I drove Mom to the new Sonic drive-in that opened down the street from them. It seems like every imaginable chain store or restaurant has opened up in the Tri-Cities since I moved away. The landscape has gone from desert to a sickening glut of consumerism. They call it expansion and growth.

We ordered root beer floats and sat in my car and talked about Dad. This is when she told me about her first husbands and how abusive they were. She explained more details about Matt's dad. She talked about Elinda and why she was sent to Medical Lake and how she got pregnant there. Then she told me what happened between Elinda and Dad.

I sat with her for about three hours, holding her hand and listening to this flood of information. These were all the things that weren't talked about when I was growing up. Stories kept from us kids.

When we were ready to leave, I tried to start my car but the battery was dead. I had kept my headlights on the whole time. I walked around and asked people in the other cars if they had jumper cables, but nobody did. Finally I asked one of the roller-skating servers and they brought out a battery charger. After a quick zap, the car started right up and we drove off, embarrassed but relieved.

The Smoking Room

The first time I went to visit Elinda after the funeral was when she had to get remarried to Chris, someone she thought she had legally married more than twenty years before. But it turned out, as I mentioned earlier, that Elinda hadn't been officially divorced from her first husband yet. She found this out when her first husband passed away with the old divorce papers, unprocessed, still in his possession.

I drove to Olympia for their small wedding at the courthouse. Mom and Mark were also there, along with a dozen other friends and relatives of Chris's. When Elinda saw me show up at the last minute, she ran over and gave me a big hug and said, "Look, everyone. My baby brother!"

During the ceremony, the judge started to go through all the various oaths. Elinda fidgeted and complained, "I just wanted to say 'I do.'"

"Well, okay then," the judge stammered.

Afterward, we went to a place called O'Malley's, a cheap family restaurant connected to a bowling alley. Dinner was a variety of chicken strips, fish and chips, and hamburgers.

I stayed with Mom and Mark at Elinda's trailer park home. The decor was as seventies as it looked from the outside, with fake-wood paneled walls, fluffy carpet, and one narrow hallway that led to two cluttered back bedrooms.

The bathroom was full of dollar-store items. In the kitchen, Elinda showed me the cupboards, packed full of boxes and cans of nonperishable food. She also had a freezer full of more food that she showed us with a proud smile.

Outside, there was a small shack at the end of the drive-way that they called the smoking room. Instead of smoking in their home, they smoked in this shack. It was just large enough for a card table, some shelves filled with board games, a TV, and a boom box. One of Elinda and Chris's friends was staying with them this same weekend and all three of them sat in the smoking room most of the night while Mom and Mark and I stayed in the trailer watching the Mariners get shellacked by the Baltimore Orioles. I looked through some photo albums that were out and kept asking Mom who people were when I didn't recognize them.

There were a couple of photos of Mom and a pretty little girl that I wondered about. "That's me with Elinda," she said. I had to stare hard at them to recognize Elinda. She was thin and happy looking, a little glint of mischief in her eyes. Probably about thirteen years old. "That was before she left," Mom said.

I turned the page and there was another picture of Elinda. In this one, she was much taller and bigger, but still young. Maybe about eighteen. She was slouched against a bench somewhere outside and her head was tilted. Her mouth was slack and open and her eyes looked faraway and helpless.

I put down the albums and went out to visit Elinda and Chris and their friend in the smoking room and noticed that there were no windows, no ventilation in the thing. At first I thought it was funny, but then I grew appalled. "You should get some windows put in this thing," I told Elinda. I felt like I was lecturing them a bit. They puffed and coughed and nodded their heads like it was old news. "Or get an air purifier or something." I could barely stand in the doorway without feeling sick. They sat in their own haze, playing cards.

That night, I slept on one of the couches in the front room. Mark slept on the other, snoring loudly. There were several lights on in the room that were keeping me awake, so I got up and turned them off. In the middle of the night, I was woken up by Elinda and her friend stumbling around and wondering if the electricity had gone out. They turned all the lights back on and went back to bed.

The next day we were at a Kmart and I looked at air purifiers, thinking I would get one for Elinda and her smoking room. Her birthday was two days away. I talked with the manager of the pharmacy area and discussed my concern with him. He told me that an air purifier would do very little to help. He said they should install some windows and fans to blow the smoke out, but even that was probably not enough. He asked how old Elinda and her husband were and I said, "About sixty."

He shook his head and said, "The best thing for them to do, really, would be to quit smoking. If they don't do that, you probably can't be too much help."

I knew he was right. I bought her oven mitts instead.

Farewell Tour

Right before Halloween 2008, I went back to Kennewick for maybe the last time in my life. Russell had convinced Mom that she should move out of the Tri-Cities finally. He was going to get her set up in San Antonio soon, near his daughter's family and closer to Houston, where Matt lives. Russell and his wife were planning to come back to Texas as well, after he was done with his current job in Korea.

My girlfriend, Barb, took the trip with me. It was a short visit and we spent part of it just driving around, looking at places from my childhood. We parked and walked around my old neighborhood and along the ditches where the floons used to be. I pointed out Willie's and Todd's old houses. We walked slowly by the house I grew up in, the house that caught fire. A woman was in the yard playing with a dog and then noticed us looking at the house. I wanted to say, "I used to live here and I'm writing a book about it." But I would have felt like a dork. Instead I just made it blatant that we were talking about their house by pointing to the window where my bedroom used to be.

We went to the Mayfair Market even though it's now called the Red Apple. Even twenty years later, I thought I might recognize someone.

We got back in the car and drove up Garfield Hill to the house that my friend Matthew grew up in and I saw that their last name was still on the mailbox. I hadn't talked to Matthew since those days in Spokane, and I wanted to go up to the door and say hello to his parents, but I chickened out.

When it got dark, we drove by my high school and saw that there was a football game going on. We stopped and snuck in the back gate and watched for an hour.

It was like a farewell tour.

Back at Mom's place, I looked through more dusty boxes of photos and artifacts. A few old letters caught my attention. There was one addressed to Mark at a correctional institute that he was in while I lived in Spokane. He had been convicted of a drug crime that I didn't know about. I also found two letters for Dad from someone named Marie who was living in Portland. They were both postmarked 1956, before he and Mom were together, but I wondered why he had kept them. They were both very romantically written and addressed to him at a place called the Welcome Hotel in Arlington, Oregon. At the bottom of one of the boxes, I was also surprised to find evidence of Dad's creative side. There were a couple drawings of horses and one of a woman's profile that looked like Judy Garland. They were pretty clean and well done, almost as if they'd been traced. But the paper was thick and Dad had signed his name on them. Some brittle papers were filled with rhyming poetry. I wondered if this was a clue to his life. If he had wanted to be an artist or a writer and just gave up hope on those things as more children and more problems piled up for him.

I was hoping I might find some older things of mine too, like the notebook of song lyrics I used to pass around in middle school. I did find a big stack of note cards with football statistics and player analyses I had written on them.

I put all the boxes back and gathered up the things I wanted to keep. Most of the boxes were old issues of motorcycle magazines that belonged to Mark.

After washing my hands, I checked out the spare room where Barb and I were supposed to sleep. It was the room where Dad had slept for the past several years, but now a friend of Mark's had taken it over. There was an overpowering cigarette stench in the air that was making our heads ache.

I asked Mom about this friend and she tried to explain that it was a woman who had been kicked out of her place and they were just letting her stay there for a while. I wasn't clear if she was Mark's girlfriend, but I figured she wasn't. Mom said that the woman was staying somewhere else that night, so we could sleep there. I looked around at this woman's stuff and saw photos of a couple of girls, presumably her daughters. There were hair clips all around the bed frame and a cheap old TV with a collection of bad movies on DVD and VHS next to it. I randomly opened a small drawer in the bedside table and immediately shut it.

"Look in there," I said to Barb.

"What is it?" she asked. She could see from my face that it was something serious. "Is it a dildo?"

I shook my head and said, "No. Worse."

She opened the drawer to see a crack pipe sitting there, not even concealed. Underneath the pipe was a letter that the woman had written, or was writing, to someone. It was a sad, pleading letter, begging someone for forgiveness. Asking for a second chance.

I put the pipe and the letter back and we decided to sleep on the living room floor instead.

Home

The next day, we went to the cemetery and found Dad's gravestone. I was surprised to see that Mom's name was on it too. I wondered if they had arranged that a long time ago. Even though they were never affectionate with each other when I was growing up and in the twenty years since I left the Tri-Cities, I guess they formed some kind of bond, or a truce that would keep them together forever. Maybe it was formed out of a mutual stubbornness, or perhaps they were used to each other, even though terrible things had happened between them. Unforgivable things. But maybe the unforgivable things were forgivable after all, for the sake of not being alone.

There were some plastic flowers at his grave. I didn't bring anything to leave. I reached down and felt the raised letters of my last name. "See you later, Dad," I said.

That night, while driving the four hours back to Portland, I realized that I probably wouldn't be coming back to Kennewick again. At least not to see any family. I will have nowhere to stay after Mom sells her place. Mark will surely stay in town after he finds a place for himself, but I doubt anyone will hear from him.

Sometimes I think about growing up in Kennewick and how normal and good it was. How I was glad that I didn't grow up in a smaller town or a bigger city. I think about my own son, growing up in Portland, and I know that his childhood, his youth, is very different. I wonder if he'll move on in a few short years and feel nostalgic later. If he'll always think of Portland as home and remember me as a good father. Maybe, right now, he thinks everything in his life is normal the way I thought my life and family was normal.

I realize that nothing is really normal. All it takes to alter normalcy is a death or a birth. Or just some misguided fear, love, or loneliness that never goes away.

Acknowledgments

Parts of this book first appeared online at *McSweeney's*, *Eleven Bulls*, *Nerve*, *Bullfight Review*, *The Glut*, *Surgery of Modern Warfare*, Powells.com, and *Smith Magazine*, and in print in *Sleepingfish* and *Igloo Zine*.

There are many people who have supported and encouraged me in my writing life. Your love and friendship mean the world to me, especially in the past two years. Thank you: Stephen Kurowski, Andrew Monko, Elizabeth Ellen, Erika Geris, Dayvid Figler, Joe O'Brien, Mike Daily, Laural Winter, Magdalen Powers, Riley Michael Parker, Gary Lutz, Pete McCracken, Reuben Nisenfeld, Melody Owen, Melissa Lion, Zachary Schomburg, Patrick deWitt, Brian Christopher, Joseph Lappie, Bob Gaulke, Melody Jordan, Ritah Parrish, Jenn Lawrence, Chelsea Martin, Martha Klein, Suzanne Burns, Emily Kendal Frey, Zoe Trope, Frank D'Andrea, and Elizabeth Miller.

Special thanks to Michael Johnson, who took some of these stories and created songs from them (long live Reclinerland).

Extra special thanks to my family for their help in piecing this together, especially: Mom, Elinda, Terry, Russell, and Matt. The good outshines the bad. John Elton Sampsell: Rest in Peace. Zacharath: I am proud that you're my son, and I hope I've learned enough to always be a good father.

Acknowledgments

For my friends at Powell's, the best bookstore in the world. Chris Faatz and Meredith Schreiber are like guardian angels. Everyone on the Publicity team (hi, Frances!) and in the Blue Room, especially Linda Watson, whose cookies and hugs have saved me a few times.

Many times to my always growing publishing-family tree. The writers I publish on Future Tense continue to inspire me. My friends at Akashic, Manic D Press, Chiasmus, and Word Riot have made me a better editor and writer.

Thanks to all the writers I've met over the years who have offered their friendship, writing secrets, blurbs, and support: Sam Lipsyte, Dan Kennedy, Miriam Toews, Jonathan Ames, Willy Vlautin, Jami Attenburg, Robin Romm, Davy Rothbart, Steve Almond, Jon Raymond, and Sean Wilsey.

Jeffrey Yamaguchi is one big reason this book exists, especially at Harper Perennial. A couple years ago, he introduced me to Carrie Kania, Amy Baker, and others at the New York office and he told them to pay attention to me, to keep me on their radar. Thanks for that push, Jeffrey. Your kindness cannot be measured.

For my agent, Michael Murphy, and my editor, Michael Signorelli—two men who were always encouraging at the right times and endlessly understanding. For Gregory Henry, Jim Hankey, and the others who help bring this book to readers.

For Barb Klansnic, you've kept me going during the hardest and most confusing times and you've elevated my happiness during exciting times. I'm lucky to have you, and I love sharing my life with you.

About the author

About the book

Insights,
Interviews
& More ...

Read on

My So-Called Real Bands

ALTHOUGH MY DREAM of being a famous DJ or pop star never came true, at least I did get to enjoy some time in a few "real bands." Here's the short list.

Drill: Drill consisted of two or three friends who would make noise behind me when I started to do spoken-word performances in Spokane in 1990.

The Girl Scout Cookies: My friend Vince from Drill decided we should try some rehearsed songs instead of just doing improv behind my poems and rants. We stole drum beats from hip hop instrumentals that Vince played guitar riffs over. We played two shows in Spokane before I moved to Arkansas in 1991.

Love Jerk: In Fort Smith, Arkansas, I became friends with two rocker kids from the local high school, and we formed a three-piece rock band. This was happening at the same time that Nirvana was hitting it big, and I was able to turn these guys on to other bands like Beat Happening and Teenage Fan Club. Phillip slashed around on his guitar, Jason pounded his drums hard (he was still into Metallica), and I tried to sing. We had one song that was an ode to Florence Henderson. We played two shows before I moved away.

Moon Boots: I reunited with Vince a couple of years later in Portland, and we decided to do a two-man band.

I played a minimalist drum kit like Moe Tucker, and he played electric guitar and sang. We played three really fun shows with actual bands that I liked, but Vince stopped smoking pot and decided that he wasn't interested anymore.

God's Favorite Pussy: This was more of a cabaret act. Five hot Portland females lip-synching to classic hits while in full costume (wigs, roller skates, Viking outfits, etc.). I was a "go-go dancer" for them. On the night that GFP opened for Deee-Lite in Portland, I stayed home tending to the early birth of my son. ∿

> ❝ We played three really fun shows with actual bands that I liked, but Vince stopped smoking pot and decided that he wasn't interested anymore. ❞

Visual Aids

HERE ARE PHOTOS and artifacts of some of the people and places that show up through the book:

This is a photo of our family home on Washington Street. I think the pillars on the front porch make it look more fancy that it really was.

Both of these photos are of Elinda, first as a little girl (probably around 1950) and the other when she was thirty-six

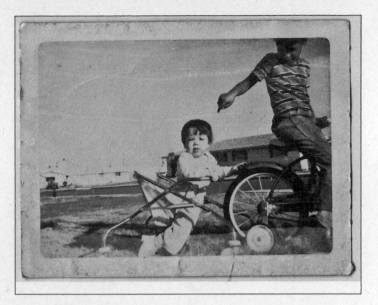

Matt towing me along in something that looks kind of dangerous. I'm always a little surprised when I see photos of me at this age because I look really chubby.

Dad when he was younger. I always thought he looked a little bit like Woody Allen. (Photo partially burned in fire.)

Visual Aids *(continued)*

Me with my friend Todd playing air guitar with crutches.

Matt with the big teenage 'fro.

Two photos of Mom, first as a beautiful young woman in the '40s and the other reading *TV Guide* in the '90s. You can see why we called her "Fuzz."

When I was home for Dad's funeral, I found a couple of photos of our house on fire. It was so odd to find these. They almost look fake. Notice the early-'70s ambulance and the gawkers.

Visual Aids *(continued)*

My dog Scooter at ten months old. Note the Cardinals sticker on the door.

Matt with his awesome green Kawasaki bike. He was the envy of the neighborhood.

A photo of the ceiling as we began installing it. This would become my favorite hiding place for porn.

This is one of those photos you find twenty years later and say, *Oh my god!* I belicve this portrait of some of the Tri-Cities New Wave crowd (circa '86) was taken at a dance somewhere. I'm in the back row, with the dangly earrings.

These are liner notes from a Neon Vomit cassette. I still have the tape if anyone wants to hear it.

Random note I found in one of Dad's boxes after the funeral.
It reads: *I am a Catholic. In case of accident please call a priest.
Thank you.*

Me (left), Stephen (middle), and Vince (right) on the
Oregon coast. A pit stop on our drive to Arkansas.

Future Tense Books
A Timeline of
My Micropress

1990: I make my first chapbook of poetry at the age of twenty-three while living in Spokane, Washington. I title it *Words of Eternal Chaos* and use the image of an old-fashioned telephone for the cover art. On the back, I decide to put *Future Tense Press.* Not knowing much about small-press publishing or zines at that time, I am more inspired by independent record labels such as Sub Pop and K Records.

1991: Using a friend's employee discount at Kinko's (and an electric typewriter), I produce three more chapbooks of my poetry (mostly sold at open mics at Auntie's Bookstore) before moving to Fort Smith, Arkansas.

1992: I decide to return to the Northwest and choose Portland, Oregon, as my new home. I start reading around town at open mics (Café Lena, Jiffy Squid) and meet other writers to publish. I buy an espresso cart business with my Arkansas girlfriend, and we call it Espresso Happening in tribute to my favorite band, Beat Happening.

1993: After the death of River Phoenix, a few friends and I write some poems to celebrate the young actor's life. We turn it into a small zine called *Dead Star.* For the next couple of years we make issues for

66 Using a friend's employee discount at Kinko's (and an electric typewriter), I produce three more chapbooks of my poetry. 99

John Candy, Charles Bukowski, John Wayne Gacy, and Elizabeth Montgomery. It's the thing I get the most mail about during this time.

I also get my first computer and P.O. box.

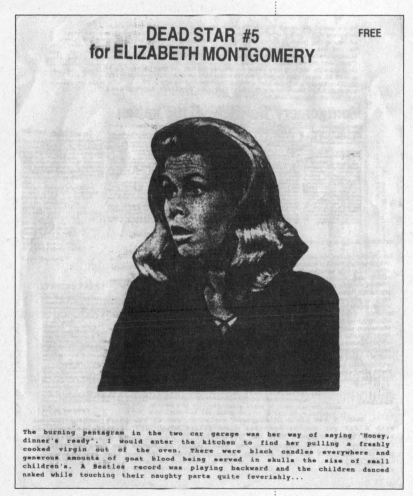

DEAD STAR #5
for ELIZABETH MONTGOMERY

FREE

The burning pentagram in the two car garage was her way of saying "Honey, dinner's ready". I would enter the kitchen to find her pulling a freshly cooked virgin out of the oven. There were black candles everywhere and generous amounts of goat blood being served in skulls the size of small children's. A Beatles record was playing backward and the children danced naked while touching their naughty parts quite feverishly...

1994: I self-publish my first paperback, *How to Lose Your Mind with the Lights On,* a collection of poems, collages, and stories—128 pages, 500 copies. It is dedicated to my son, Zach, who is born in July.

Another paperback release, by performance artist Drew Pisarra, comes out a few months later.

1995: At a local café called Umbra Penumbra, I start the Future Tense reading series for writers I publish and other friends.

1996: My first stab at a themed collection, *The Diner Anthology,* is released as a chapbook and includes an array of '90s small-press stars.

1997: I publish a collection of poems, *Jesus Christ: Live and In the Flesh,* by "queen of the small press," Lyn Lifshin.

My life becomes a shambles after I split with my son's mom. On a somewhat related note, I become unspoken enemies with writer Jim Goad when my homewrecker girlfriend starts dating him.

I begin working at Powell's as "Christmas help" and become events coordinator less than a year later.

I get married to writer and performer Ritah Parrish at a pajama party reading at a tiki bar. Many people don't believe it's real, but we stay married for five years.

(Note to reader: Someday, when I write another memoir, it will probably start in 1997.)

> 66 I get married to writer and performer Ritah Parrish at a pajama party reading at a tiki bar. Many people don't believe it's real, but we stay married for five years. 99

1998: The first Future Tense website is launched. It's a big, garish yellow thing with a grenade on its front page. It eventually gets made over, with a sleek black and white design.

We win our first Oregon Literary Arts fellowship.

1999: A chapbook *(Holes)* by legendary rock writer Richard Meltzer is released. It consists of a funny essay on golf and a section of poems.

2000: Our first novel, *Meat Won't Pay My Light Bill* by artist and bartender Kurt Eisenlohr, is released. Because of its size (240 pages), I can only afford to print 300 copies. The book goes out of print quickly until being republished in 2008 by another press. (Kurt's connection to Future Tense remains: his art adorns our website.)

Jemiah Jefferson's chapbook of stories, *St*rf*ck*ng,* is released. She goes on to write several acclaimed vampire novels.

Business-wise, I finally decide to make some kind of letterhead.

2001: We publish *Please Don't Kill the Freshman* by Zoe Trope, a girl I discover in an eighth-grade after-school writing class I taught in 1999. The 44-page book, a diary of her first year in high school, becomes a local sensation and is bought by Harper Tempest. An expanded version of her book comes out in 2003. The chapbook is the bestselling title I've ever published.

> 66 We publish *Please Don't Kill the Freshman* by Zoe Trope, a girl I discover in an eighth-grade after-school writing class I taught in 1999. . . . The chapbook is the bestselling title I've ever published. 99

Future Tense Books *(continued)*

2002: Another Future Tense release, *Grosse Pointe Girl* by Sarah Grace McCandless, a book edited by Ritah (who also has two books released on Future Tense), is bought by Simon & Schuster.

Ritah and I get divorced.

The first version of *A Common Pornography* comes out. I start corresponding with a girl named Barb, who reads parts of the book on the *McSweeney's* website.

2003: Barb moves from Los Angeles to Portland, and romance blooms. She moves into "Future Tense Headquarters."

Haiku Inferno—a "performance group" consisting of me, Barb (a.k.a. Frayn Masters), Elizabeth Miller, and Frank D'Andrea—debuts and performs at various events for the next several years. A book (copublished by Future Tense and Portland's Crack Press) comes out five years later.

Controversial sex writer Susannah Breslin's book, *You're a Bad Man, Aren't You?*, comes out in a limited paperback release and quickly sells out.

Happy Ending by Mike Topp, our first New York writer, is released.

We also win our second Literary Arts fellowship this year.

2004: I bravely try my hand at a special fold-out chapbook, a collection of dirty poems by Shane Allison called *Black Fag*. It's a tricky production (and maybe not entirely successful due to my folding), but it becomes a hit among queer poetry fans.

2005: I team up with legendary San Francisco publisher Manic D Press to start a paperback imprint through them, simply called the Future Tense series. An anthology, *The Insomniac Reader,* is the first release.

2006: *Fast Forward: Confessions of a Porn Screenwriter* by *Playboy* writer and *Believer* editor Eric Spitznagel is the second book copublished with Manic D Press.

A chapbook by Tao Lin is scheduled for summer before I pull the plug on the project due to editing concerns. The resulting ballyhoo is discussed heatedly on lit blogs for the rest of the year before Tao moves on to Melville House (we've since become friendly again).

2007: *Dahlia Season* by Myriam Gurba, the third book through Manic D Press, wins the Edmund White Award for Debut Fiction.

Elizabeth Ellen's debut, *Before You She Was a Pit Bull,* comes out to the delight of short story fans.

After many years of e-mailing about it, *Partial List of People to Bleach,* a chapbook by Gary Lutz (who is probably my favorite writer ever), is released.

Also after many years, we finally unveil a logo: a long stapler image.

> **66** After many years, we finally unveil a logo: a long stapler image. **99**

Future Tense Books *(continued)*

2008: After many years of criticizing the shoddy print-on-demand industry, I realize that it has vastly improved and become more accessible—no more 300-copy print runs! Bob Gaulke's humorous book on teaching English in Japan, *Embrace Your Insignificance,* is released.

I meet a young man named Riley Michael Parker at Powell's and give him some book recommendations. A couple of months later, he gives me a short manuscript that blindsides me. I quickly halt everything else to turn it into a chapbook *(Our Beloved 26th).*

2009: Oakland writer and artist Chelsea Martin releases *Everything Was Fine Until Whatever,* our second paperback in a year. It becomes the fastest-selling paperback we've ever done.

To learn more about Kevin's micropress, go to www.futuretensebooks.com. ❧